Elijah and the Secret of His Power

A Biblical Biography of the Old Testament –
Elias, Prophet of God

By F. B. Meyer

Logo art adapted from work by Bernard Gagnon

ISBN-13: 978-0-359-73312-5

First published in 1901

Contents

Chapter One - The Source of Elijah's Strength

This chapter begins with the conjunction "And." It is, therefore, an addition to what has gone before; and it is God's addition. When we have read to the end of the previous chapter -- which tells the melancholy story of the rapid spread and universal prevalence of idolatry in the favored land of the ten tribes of Israel -- we might suppose that that was the end of all; and that the worship of Jehovah would never again acquire its lost prestige and power. And, no doubt, the principal actors in the story thought so too. Ahab thought so, Jezebel thought so, the false prophets thought so, the scattered remnant of hidden disciples thought so.

But they had made an unfortunate omission in their calculations -- they had left out Jehovah Himself. He must have something to say at such a crisis. He must add a few chapters before the history is closed. When men have done their worst and finished, it is the time for God to begin. And when God begins, He is likely, with one blow, to reverse all that has been done without Him; and to write some pages of human history which will be a lesson and an inspiration to all coming time. That "And" is ominous enough to His foes; but it is full of hope and promise to His friends.

Things were dark enough. After the death of Solomon, his kingdom split into two parts. The southern was under Rehoboam, his son; the northern under Jeroboam, who had superintended the vast public works. Jeroboam was desperately eager to keep his hold on his people; but he feared to sole it if they continued to go, two or three times a year, to the annual feasts at Jerusalem. He thought that old associations might overpower their newborn loyalty to himself. He resolved, therefore, to set up the worship of Jehovah in his own territories, and erected two temples, one at Dan, in the extreme north, the other at Bethel, in the extreme south. And in each of these places he placed a golden calf, that the God of Israel might be worshipped "under the form of a calf that eateth hay." This sin broke the second commandment -- which forbade the children of Israel to make any graven image or to bow down before the likeness of anything in heaven above, or in the earth beneath. So weak and sinful a bid for popularity is never forgotten in Holy Scripture. Like a funeral knell, the words ring out again and again: "Jeroboam, the son of Nebat, who made Israel to sin."

After many revolutions and much bloodshed, the kingdom passed into the hands of a military adventurer, Omri. The son of this man was Ahab, who "did more to provoke the Lord God of Israel to anger than all the kings of Israel that were before him" (1Ki_16:33). This came to pass, not so much because his character was more depraved, but because he was a weak man, the tool of a crafty, unscrupulous, and cruel woman. Some of the worst crimes that have ever been committed have been wrought by weak men at the instigation of worse -- but stronger -- spirits than themselves.

When the young and beautiful Jezebel left the ceiled palaces of Tyre to become the consort of the newly-crowned king of Israel, it was no doubt regarded as a splendid match. At that time Tyre sat as queen upon the seas in the zenith of her glory. Her colonies dotted the shores of the Mediterranean as far as Spain. Her ships whitened every sea with their sails, and ventured to the coasts of our own Cornwall for tin. Her daughter, Carthage, nursed the lion cub Hannibal, and was strong enough to make Rome tremble. But, like many a splendid match, it was fraught with misery and disaster. No one can disobey God's plain words against intermarriage with the ungodly without suffering for it at last.

As she left her palace home, Jezebel would be vehemently urged by the priests -- beneath whose influence she had been trained, and who, therefore, exercised an irresistible spell over her -- to do her utmost to introduce into Israel the hideous and cruel rites of her hereditary religion. Nor was she slow to obey. First, she seems to have erected a temple to Astarte in the neighborhood of Jezreel, the Windsor of the land, and to have supported its four hundred and fifty priests from the revenues of her private purse. Then Ahab and she built a temple for Baal in Samaria, the capital of the kingdom, large enough to contain immense crowds of worshipers (1Ki_16:32). Shrines and temples then began to rise in all parts of the land in honor of these false deities; while the altars of Jehovah, like that at Carmel, were ruthlessly broken down. The land swarmed with the priests of Baal and of the groves -- proud of court favor; glorying in their sudden rise to power; insolent, greedy, licentious, and debased. The fires of persecution were lit and began to burn with fury. The schools of the prophets were shut up, and grass grew in their courts. The prophets themselves were hunted down and slain by the sword. They wandered about in sheepskins and goatskins, being destitute, afflicted, tormented. The pious Obadiah had great difficulty in saving a few of them by hiding them in the limestone caves of Carmel and feeding them at the risk of his own life.

The whole land seemed apostate. Of all the thousands of Israel, only seven thousand remained who had not bowed the knee or kissed the hand to Baal. But they were paralyzed with fear and kept so still that their very existence was unknown by Elijah in the hour of his greatest loneliness. Such times have often come, fraught with woe: false religions have gained the upper hand, iniquity has abounded, and the love of many has waxed cold. So was it when the Turk swept over the Christian communities of Asia Minor and replaced the cross by the crescent. So was it when Roman Catholicism spread over Europe as a pall of darkness that grew denser as the dawn of the Reformation was on the point of breaking. So it was in the last century, when moderatism reigned in Scotland, and apathy in England.

But God is never at a loss. The land may be overrun with sin, the lamps of witness may seem all extinguished, the whole force of the popular current may run counter to His truth, and the plot may threaten to be within a hair's breadth of entire success, but all the time He will be preparing a weak man in some obscure highland village, and in the moment of greatest need will send him forth, as His all-sufficient answer to the worst plottings of His foes. "When the enemy shall come in like a flood, the Spirit of the Lord shall lift up a standard against him" (Isa_59:19 b). So it has been, and so it shall be again.

Elijah was an in habitant of Gilead. Gilead lay east of the Jordan. It was wild and rugged, its hills were covered with shaggy forests, its awful solitudes were only broken by the dash of mountain streams, and its valleys were the haunt of fierce wild beasts. What the highlands of Argyleshire and Inverness were a century ago to the lowland towns of Scotland, that must Gilead have been to the more refined and civilized people of Jerusalem and Samaria. The inhabitants of Gilead partook of the character of their country -- wild, lawless, and unkempt. They lived in rude stone villages and subsisted by keeping flocks of sheep.

Elijah grew up like the other lads of his age. In his early years he probably did the work of a shepherd on those wild hills. As he grew to manhood, his erect figure, his shaggy locks, his cloak of camel's hair, his muscular, sinewy strength -- which could out strip the fiery coursers of the royal chariot and endure excessive physical fatigue -- distinguished him from the dwellers in lowland valleys. But in none of these would he be specially different from the men who grew up with him in the obscure mountain hamlet of Thisbe, whence he derived the name of Tishbite. There were many among them as lithe, and swift, and strong, and capable of fatigue, as he. We must not look to these things for the secret of his strength.

As he grew in years, he became characterized by an intense religious earnestness. He was "very jealous for the Lord God of hosts." Deeply taught in Scripture, especially in those passages which told how much

Jehovah had done for His people, Elijah yearned, with passionate desire, that they should give Him His meed of honor. And he learned that this was lacking by the dread tidings that came in broken snatches. Messengers after messenger told how Jezebel had thrown down God's altars and slain His prophets and replaced them by the impious rites of her Tyrian deities -- his blood ran liquid fire, his indignation burst all bounds, he was "very jealous for the Lord God of hosts." O noble heart! I wish that we could be as righteously indignant amid the evils of our time! Oh for a coal from that pure flame that burnt on thine inner hearth!

But the question was, How should he act? What could he do -- a wild, untutored child of the desert? There was only one thing he could do -- the resource of all much-tried souls -- he could pray, and he did: "He prayed earnestly" (Jas_5:17). And in his prayer he seems to have been led back to a denunciation made years before by Moses to the people -- that if they turned aside and served other gods, and worshiped them, the Lord's wrath would be kindled against them; and He would shut up the heaven so there should be no rain (Deu_11:16-17). Flowing into this mold, his thoughts must have shaped themselves somewhat thus: "If my God does not fulfill this threat the people will think that it is an idle tale, or that He is a myth of the past -- a dead tradition. This must not be. Better far that the land should suffer the terrors of famine, and the people experience the bitterest agonies of thirst, and that I should be torn limb from limb. It were better that we should suffer the direst physical woes that can blast our national prosperity, than that we should come to think that the Jehovah of our fathers is as dead as the idols of the heathen." And so he set himself to pray that the terrible threat might be literally fulfilled. "He prayed earnestly that it might not rain."

A terrible prayer indeed! And yet, was it not more terrible for the people to forget and ignore the God of their fathers, and to give themselves up to the licentious orgies of Baal and Astarte? Remember, too, what a wrong construction might be put upon the utter silence of God Himself. Could anything be more disastrous than that the statute book should be filled with laws which the Lawgiver could not or would not enforce? Nothing could be more detrimental to the true conception of God. "These things hast thou done, and I kept silence; thou thoughtest that I was altogether such an one as thyself: but I will reprove thee and set them in order before thine eyes" (Psa_50:21).

Physical suffering is a smaller calamity than moral delinquency. And the love of God does not shrink from inflicting such suffering, if, as a result, the plague of sin may be cut out as a cancer and stayed. It may be that this is why there is so much sorrow in life. One may be suffering a terrible drought, before which all the springs of his prosperity are drying up. No dews of grace or rains of blessing have fallen on one's lot for many days. This is not a chance; it is the work of One who loves His own too well to permit him to forsake Himself without making one effort to arrest and change a life. The cornfield is fired only because He wants to bring him to Himself (2Sa_14:30). The drought is sent only to enforce the rebuilding of the altar on Carmel's height and the immolation of the false priests in the vale beneath.

And as Elijah prayed, the conviction was wrought into his mind that it should be even as he prayed; and that he should go to acquaint Ahab with the fact. Whatever might be the hazard to himself, both king and people must be made to connect their calamities with the true cause. And this they evidently did, as we shall see (1Ki_18:10). That the drought was due to his prayer is also to be inferred from the express words with which Elijah announced the fact to the king: "There shall not be dew nor rain these years, but according to my word" (1Ki_17:1).

What a meeting was that! We know not where it took place, whether in the summer palace when Jezebel was at her consort's side, or when Ahab was surrounded by his high officers of state in Samaria. But wherever it took place, it was a subject worthy of the highest art and genius. The old religion against the new; the child of nature against the flaccid child of courts; camel's hair against soft clothing; moral strength against moral weakness.

This interview needed no ordinary moral strength. It was no child's play for the untutored man of the desert to go on such an errand to that splendid court! What chance was there of his escaping with his life? Surely he would not fare better than the prophets who had not dared so much as he! Yet he came and went unhurt, in the panoply of a might which seemed invulnerable.

What was the secret of that strength? If it can be shown that it was due to something inherent in Elijah and peculiar to himself; some force of nature, some special quality of soul to which ordinary men can lay no claim; then we may as well close our inquiries and turn away from the inaccessible heights that mock us. But if it can be shown, as I think it can, that this splendid life was lived not by its inherent qualities, but by sources of strength which are within the reach of the humblest child of God who reads these lines, then every line of it is an inspiration, beckoning us to its own glorious level. Courage, brothers! There is nothing in this man's life which may not have its counterpart in ours, if only it can be established that his strength was obtained from sources which are accessible to ourselves.

Elijah's strength did not lie in himself or his surroundings. He was of humble extraction. He had no special training. He is expressly said to have been "a man of like passions" with ourselves. When, through failure of faith, he was cut off from the source of his strength, he showed more craven-hearted cowardice than most men would have done. He lay down upon the desert sands, asking to die. When the natural soil of his nature shows itself, it is not richer than that of the majority of men. If anything it is the reverse.

Elijah gives us three indications of the source of his strength.

1. "AS JEHOVAH LIVETH."

To all beside, Jehovah might seem dead; but to him He was the one supreme reality of life. And if we would be strong, we too must be able to say, "I know that my redeemer liveth" (Job_19:25), "He ever liveth to make intercession for us" (Heb_7:25), and "because he lives, we shall live also" (Joh_14:19). The death of the cross was bitter, but He lives. The spear made fearful havoc, but He lives. The grave was fast closed, but He lives. Men and devils did their worst, but He lives. The man who has heard Jesus say, "I am he that liveth" (Rev_1:18), will also hear Him say, "Fear not! be strong, yea, be strong."

2. "BEFORE WHOM I STAND."

He was standing in the presence of Ahab; but he was conscious of the presence of a greater than any earthly monarch, the presence of Jehovah, before whom angels bow in lowly worship, harkening to the voice of His word. Gabriel himself could not employ a loftier designation (Luk_1:19). Let us cultivate this habitual recognition of the presence of God, it will lift us above all other fear. Let us build our cottage so that every window may look out on the mighty Alps of God's presence; and that we may live, and move, and have our being beneath the constant impression that God is here. Besides this, a conviction had been borne in upon his mind that he was chosen by God to be His called and recognized servant and messenger; and in this capacity he stood before Him.

3. "JEHOVAH IS MY STRENGTH."

The word ELIJAH may be rendered "Jehovah is my God," but there is another possible translation, "Jehovah is my strength." This gives the key to Elijah's life. God was the strength of his life; of whom should he be afraid? When the wicked, even his enemies and foes, came on him to eat up his flesh, they stumbled and fell. Though an host should encamp against him, his heart should not fear. What a revelation is given us in this name! Oh that it were true of each of us! Yet, why should it not be? Let us from henceforth cease from our own strength, which at the best is weakness; and let us appropriate God's by daily, hourly faith. Then this shall be the motto of our future lives: "In the LORD have I righteousness and strength" (Isa_45:24), "I can do all things through Christ which strengtheneth me" (Php_4:13), "the LORD is my strength and song, and is become my salvation" (Psa_118:14).

Chapter Two - Beside the Drying Brook

We are studying the life of a man of like passions with ourselves, one who was weak where we are weak, failing where we would fail. But he stood, single-handed, against his people and stemmed the tide of idolatry and sin and turned a nation back to God. And he did it by the use of resources which are within reach of us all. This is the fascination of the story. If it can be proven that he acted under a spell of some secret which is hidden from us ordinary persons or that he was cast in an heroic mold to which we can lay no claim, then disappointment will overcast our interest and we must lay aside the story. Elijah would be a model we could not copy, an ideal we could not realize, a vision that mocks us as it fades into the azure of the past.

But this is not the case. This man, by whom God threshed the mountains, was only a worm at the best. This pillar in God's temple was, by nature, a reed shaken by the breath of the slightest zephyr. This prophet of fire who shone like a torch, was originally but a piece of smoking flax. Faith made him all he became, and faith will do as much for us if only we can exercise it to appropriate the might of the eternal God as he did. All power is in God, and it has pleased Him to store it all in the risen Savior, as in some vast reservoir. These stores are brought into human hearts by the Holy Ghost, and the Holy Ghost is given according to the measure of our receptivity and faith. Oh, for Elijah's receptiveness, that we might be as full of Divine power as he was, and as able, therefore, to do exploits for God and truth!

But, before this can happen, we must pass through the same education as he. You must go to Cherith and Zarephath before you can stand on Carmel. Even the faith you have must be pruned, educated, and matured so that it may become strong enough to subdue kingdoms, work righteousness, and turn armies of aliens to flight.

Notice, then, the successive steps in God's education of His servants.

1. GOD'S SERVANTS MUST LEARN TO TAKE ONE STEP AT A TIME.

This is an elementary lesson, but it is hard to learn. No doubt Elijah found it so. Before he left Thisbe for Samaria, to deliver the message that burdened his soul, he would naturally inquire what he should do when he had delivered it. How would he be received? What would be the outcome? Where should he go to escape the vengeance of Jezebel, who had not shrunk from slaying the prophets less dauntless than himself? If he had asked those questions of God and waited for a reply before he left his highland home, he would never have gone at all. Our Father never treats His children so. He only shows us one step at a time, and He bids us take it in faith. If we look up into His face and say: "But if I take this step which is certain to involve me in difficulty, what shall I do next?" the heavens will be mute save with the one repeated message, "Take it and trust Me."

But directly God's servant took the step to which he was led, and delivered the message, then "the word of the Lord came to him, saying: Get thee hence, ...hide thyself by the brook Cherith" (1Ki_17:3). So it was afterwards; it was only when the brook had dried up, and the stream had dwindled to pools, and the pools to drops, and the drops had died away in the sand -- only then did the word of the Lord come to him, saying, "Arise, get thee to Zarephath" (1Ki_17:9).

I like that phrase, "the word of the Lord came to him." He did not need to go to search for it; it came to him. And so it will come to you. It may come through the Word of God, or through a distinct impression made on your heart by the Holy Ghost, or through circumstances; but it will find you out, and tell you what you are to do. "Lord, what wilt thou have me to do? And the Lord said unto him, Arise and go into the city, and it shall be told thee what thou must do" (Act_9:6).

 It may be that for long you have had upon your mind some strong impression of duty; but you have held back, because you could not see what the next step would be. Hesitate no longer. Step out upon what seems to be the impalpable mist, and you will find a slab of adamant beneath your feet. Every time you put your foot forward, you will find that God has prepared a stepping-stone, and another, and another; each appearing as you come to it. The bread is by the day. The manna is every morning. The strength is according to the moment's need. God does not give all the directions at once, lest we should get confused. He tells us just as much as we can remember and do. Then we must look to Him for more. So we learn, by easy stages, the sublime habits of obedience and trust.

2. GOD'S SERVANTS MUST BE TAUGHT THE VALUE OF THE HIDDEN LIFE.

"Get thee hence and turn thee eastward, and hide thyself by the brook Cherith" (1Ki_17:3). The man who is to take a high place before his fellows must take a low place before his God, and there is no better manner of bringing a man down than by suddenly dropping him out of a sphere to which he was beginning to think himself essential, teaching him that he is not at all necessary to God's plan, and compelling him to consider in the sequestered vale of some Cherith how miked are his motives, and how insignificant his strength.

So the Master dealt with His apostles. When, on one occasion, they returned to Him, full of themselves and flushed with success, He quietly said, "Come ye yourselves apart into a desert place." We are too strong, too full of self, for God to use us. We vainly imagine that we are something, and that God cannot dispense with us. How urgently we need that God should bury our self-centeredness in the darkness of a Cherith or a tomb, so as to hide it, and keep it in the place of death. We must not be surprised, then, if sometimes our Father says: "There, child, you have had enough of this hurry, and publicity, and excitement; go and hide yourself by the brook -- hide yourself in the Cherith of the sick chamber, or in the Cherith of bereavement, or in some solitude from which the crowds have ebbed away." Happy is he who can reply, "This Your will is also mine; I flee to You to hide me. Hide me in the secret of Your tabernacle, and beneath the cover of Your wings!"

Every saintly soul that would wield great power with men must win it in some hidden Cherith. A Carmel triumph always presupposes a Cherith; and a Cherith always leads to a Carmel. We cannot give out unless we have previously taken in. We cannot exorcise the devils unless we have first entered into our closets and shut our doors and spent hours of rapt intercourse with God. The acquisition of spiritual power is impossible, unless we hide ourselves from men and from ourselves in some deep gorge where we may absorb the power of the eternal God; as vegetation through long ages absorbed these qualities of sunshine which it gives back through burning coal.

Bishop Andrewes had his Cherith in which he spent five hours every day in prayer and devotion. John Welsh, who thought the day ill-spent which did not witness eight or ten hours of closet communion, had it. David Brainard had it in the woods of North America, which were the favorite scene of his devotions. Christmas Evans had it in his long and lonely journeys amid the hills of Wales. Fletcher of Madeley, who would often leave his classroom for his private chamber and spend hours upon his knees with his students, pleading for the fullness of the Spirit till they could kneel no longer, had his Cherith. Or, passing back to the blessed age from which we date the centuries, Patmos, the seclusion of the Roman prisons, the Arabian desert, and the hills and vales of Palestine, are forever memorable as the Cheriths of those who have made our modern world. Our Lord found His Cherith at Nazareth, in the wilderness of Judea, amid the olives of Bethany, and in the solitudes of Gadara. Not one of

12

us can dispense with some Cherith where the sounds of earthly toil and human voices are exchanged for the murmur of the waters of quietness which are fed from the throne and where we may taste the sweets and imbibe the power of a life hidden in Christ by the power of the Holy Ghost. Sometimes a human spirit, intent on its quest, may even find its Cherith in a crowd. For such an one, God is an all-sufficient abode, and the secret place of the Most High is its most holy place.

3. GOD'S SERVANTS MUST LEARN TO TRUST GOD ABSOLUTELY.

At first we yield a timid obedience to a command which seems to involve manifest impossibilities; but when we find that God is even better than His word, our faith grows exceedingly, and we advance to further feats of faith and service. This is how God trains His young eaglets to fly. At last nothing is impossible. This is the key to Elijah's experience.

How strange to be sent to a brook, which would of course be as subject to the drought as any other! How contrary to nature to suppose that ravens, which feed on carrion, would find such food as man could eat; or, having found it, would bring it regularly morning and evening! How unlikely, too, that he could remain secreted from the search of the bloodhounds of Jezebel anywhere within the limits of Israel! But God's command was clear and unmistakable. It left him no alternative but to obey. "So he went and did according to the word of the Lord" (1Ki_17:5).

One evening, as we may imagine, Elijah reached the narrow gorge, down which the brook bounded with musical babble toward the Jordan. On either side the giant cliffs towered up, inclosing a little patch of blue sky. The interlacing boughs of the trees made a natural canopy in the hottest noon. All along the streamlet's course the moss would make a carpet of richer hue and softer texture than could be found in the palaces of kings. And, yonder, came the ravens -- "the ravens brought him bread and flesh in the morning... [and] in the evening" (1Ki_17:6). What a lesson was this of God's power to provide for his child! In after days, Elijah would often recur to it as dating a new epoch in his life. "I can never doubt God again. I am thankful that He shut me off from all other supplies, and threw me back on Himself. I am sure that He will never fail me, whatsoever the circumstances of strait or trial through which He may call me to pass."

There is a strong emphasis on the word THERE -- "I have commanded the ravens to feed thee there" (1Ki_17:4). Elijah might have preferred many hiding places to Cherith; but that was the only place to which the ravens would bring his supplies; and, as long as he wan there, God was pledged to provide for him. Our supreme thought should be: "Am I where God wants me to be?" If so, God will work a direct miracle rather than

13

suffer us to perish for lack. If the younger son chooses to go to the far country of his own accord, he may be in danger of dying of starvation among his swine; but if the Father sends him there, he shall have enough and to spare. God sends no soldier to the warfare on his own charges. He does not expect us to attend to the duties of the field and the commissariat. The manna always accompanies the pillar of cloud. If we do His will on earth as in heaven, He will give us daily bread. "Seek ye first the kingdom of God and his righteousness, and all these shall be added unto you" (Mat_6:33).

We will not stay to argue the probability of this story being true. It is enough that it is written here. And the presence of the supernatural presents no difficulties to those who can say "Our Father," and who believe in the resurrection of our Lord Jesus. But if corroboration were needed, it could be multiplied an hundred-fold from the experience of living people, who have had their needs supplied in ways quite as marvelous as the coming of ravens to the lonely prophet.

A little boy, having read this incident with his widowed mother one wintry night, as they sat in a fireless room beside a bare table, asked her if he might set the door open for God's ravens to come in; he was so sure that they must be on their way. The burgomaster of that German town, passing by, was attracted by the sight of the open door, and entered, inquiring the cause. When he learned the reason, he said, "I will be God's raven," and relieved their need then and afterward. Ah, reader, God has an infinite fertility of resource; and if thou art doing His work where He would have thee, He will supply thy need, though the heavens fall. Only trust Him!

4. GOD'S SERVANTS ARE OFTEN CALLED TO SIT BY DRYING BROOKS.

"It came to pass after a while, that the brook dried up" (1Ki_17:7). Our wildest fancy can but inadequately realize the condition to which the Land of Promise was reduced by the first few months of drought. The mountain pastures were seared as by the passage of fire. The woodlands and copses were scorched and silent. The rivers and brooks shrank attenuated in their beds, receding continually, and becoming daily more shallow and still. There was no rain to revive vegetation or replenish the supplies of water. The sun rose and set for months in the sky, the blue of which was unflecked by a single cloud. There was no dew to sprinkle the parched, cracked earth with refreshing tears. And so Cherith began to sing less cheerily. Each day marked a visible diminution of its stream. Its voice grew fainter and fainter till its bed became a course of stones, baking in the scorching heat. It dried up.

What did Elijah think? Did he think that God had forgotten him? Did he begin to make plans for himself? This would have been human; but we will hope that he waited quietly for God, quieting himself as a weaned child, as he sang, "My soul, wait thou only upon God; for my expectation is from him" (Psa_62:5).

Many of us have had to sit by drying brooks. Perhaps some are sitting by them now -- the drying brook of popularity which is ebbing away as from John the Baptist; the drying brook of health, sinking under a creeping paralysis, or a slow consumption; the drying brook of money, slowly dwindling before the demands of sickness, bad debts, or other people's extravagance; the drying brook of friendship, which for long has been diminishing and threatens soon to cease. Ah, it is hard to sit beside a drying brook, much harder than to face the prophets of Baal on Carmel.

Why does God let them dry? He wants to teach us not to trust in His gifts, but in Himself. He wants to drain us of self, as He drained the apostles by ten days of waiting before Pentecost. He wants to loosen our roots before He removes us to some other sphere of service and education. He wants to put in stronger contrast the river of throne-water that never dries. Let us learn these lessons, and turn from our failing Cheriths to our unfailing Savior. All sufficiency resides in Him -- unexhausted by the flight of the ages, undiminished by the thirst of myriads of saints. The river of God is full of water. "Whosoever drinketh of this water shall thirst again: But whosoever drinketh of the water that I shall give him shall be in him a well of water springing up into everlasting life" (Joh_4:13-14). "Drink abundantly, O beloved!" (Son_5:1).

Chapter Three - Ordered to Zarephath

A friend of mine, spending a few days in the neighborhood of our English lakes, came upon the most beautiful shrubs he had ever seen. Arrested by their extraordinary luxuriance, he inquired the cause and learned that it was due to a judicious system of transplanting, constantly pursued. Whatever may be the effect of such a process in nature, it is certainly true that our heavenly Father employs similar methods to secure the highest results in us. He is constantly transplanting us. And though these changes threaten at times to hinder all steady progress in the spiritual life, if they are rightly borne they result in the most exquisite manifestations of Christian character and experience.

Another illustration of the same truth is given by the prophet Jeremiah, when he says, "Moab hath been at ease from his youth, and he hath

15

settled on his lees, and hath not been emptied from vessel to vessel, neither hath he gone into captivity: therefore his taste remained in him, and his scent is not changed" (Jer_48:11). Grape juice, when first expressed from its ruddy chalice, is impure and thick. It is left in vessels until fermentation has done its work, and a thick sediment, called lees, has been precipitated to the bottom. When this is done, the liquid is carefully drawn off into another vessel, so that all the precipitated sediment is left behind. This emptying process is repeated again and again, till the offensive odor that came from the lees has passed away, and the liquid has become clear and beautiful. In the case of Moab there had been none of this unsettling process, and consequently the people had made no moral or spiritual progress; his taste remained in him, and his scent [was] not changed" (Jer_48:11). The quiet life is by no means the greatest life. Some characters can only reach the highest standard of spirituality by the disturbings or displacings in the order of God's providence.

Will not this cast light upon God's dealings with Elijah? Once he stood in the vessel "home;" then emptied into the vessel "Jezreel;" then into the vessel "Cherith;" and now into the fourth vessel, "Zarephath." All this that he might not settle upon his lees, but be urged toward a goal of moral greatness which he otherwise would never have reached. This qualified him to take his stand on the Transfiguration Mount as the associate of Moses and the companion of Christ. Take heart, you who are compelled to be constantly on the move -- pitching the tent tonight, only to be summoned by the moving cloud and the trumpet call to strike it tomorrow. All this is under the direction of a wise and faithful love which is educating you for a glorious destiny. Believe only that your circumstances are those most suited to develop your character. They have been selected out of all possible combinations of events and conditions in order to effect in you the highest finish of usefulness and beauty. They would have been the ones selected by you if all the wide range of omniscient knowledge had been within your reach.

And yet, when a human spirit is entirely taken up with God as Elijah was, these changes become comparatively harmless and trifling -- as a gnat sting to a soldier in the heat of battle. To one who lives in the presence of the unchanging God and who can say, "Thus saith Jehovah, before whom I stand," the ever-varying conditions of our lot touch only the outer rim of life. Whatever they take away, they cannot take THAT away. Whatever they bring, they cannot give more than THAT. The consciousness of that Presence is the one all- mastering thought -- the inspiration, the solace, the comfort, of every waking hour. And as we have seen a far-spread summer landscape through the haze of intense heat, so do all

16

people and things and events show themselves through the all-enwrapping, all- encompassing presence of God. To fulfill His plans, to obey the least intimation of His will, to wait on His hand, to dwell in the absorbing vision of Himself, to be satisfied with the fullness of joy which fills His presence-chamber with sweetest perfume and with celestial music -- this is the one passion of the happy spirit, to whom, as to Elijah, this grace is given. But such grace is for you, through the Holy Ghost, if only you will open to it all the capacities of your heart and life. Why not seek it?

There are several lessons here.

Faith Awaits God's Plans

"It came to pass, after a while, that the brook dried up, because there had been no rain in the land." Week after week, with unfaltering and steadfast spirit, Elijah watched that dwindling brook; often tempted to stagger through unbelief, but refusing to allow his circumstances to come between himself and God. Unbelief sees God through circumstances, as we sometimes see the sun shorn of its rays through the smoky air; but faith puts God between itself and circumstances, and looks at them through Him. And so the dwindling brook became a silver thread, and the silver thread stood presently in pools at the foot of the largest boulders, and then the pools shrank. The birds fled, the wild creatures of field and forest came no more to drink, the brook was dry. Only then, to his patient and unwavering spirit, "the word of the Lord came unto him, saying, Arise, get thee to Zarephath" (1Ki_7:8-9).

Most of us would have become anxious and worn with planning long before that. We should have ceased our songs as soon as the streamlet caroled less musically over its rocky bed. With harps swinging on the willows we should have paced to and fro upon the withering grass, lost in pensive thought. And probably, long before the brook was dry, we should have devised some plan, and asking God's blessing on it, would have started off elsewhere. Alas! we are all too full of our own schemes, and plans, and contrivings. And if Samuel does not come just when we expect, we force ourselves and offer the burnt-offering (1Sa_13:12). This is the source of the untold misery. We sketch out our program and rush into it. Only when we are met by insuperable obstacles do we begin to reflect whether it was God's will or to appeal to Him. He does often extricate us because His mercy endureth forever, but if we had only waited first to see the unfolding of His plans, we should never have found ourselves landed in such an inextricable labyrinth. We should never have been compelled to retrace our steps with so many tears of shame.

One of the formative words for all human lives, and especially for God's servants, was given by God to Moses, when He said, "See... that thou make all things according to the pattern showed to thee in the mount" (Heb_8:5). Moses was eager to do God's work, and the best skill among the people was at his command; but he must not make a single bell, pomegranate, tassel, fringe, curtain, or vessel, except on God's pattern and after God's ideal. And so he was taken up into the mount, and God opened the door into His own mind where the tabernacle stood complete as an ideal; and Moses was permitted to see the thing as it lived in the thought and heart of God. Forty days of reverent study passed by. When Moses returned to the foot of the mountain, he had only to transfer into the region of actual fact that which had been already shown to him, in pattern, on the mount.

Surely some such thought as this must have been in the mind of our blessed Lord, when He said, "The Son can do nothing of himself, but what he seeth the Father do" (Joh_5:19). So utterly had He emptied Himself that He had abandoned even His own schemes and plans. He lived a planless life, accepting each moment the plan which His Father unfolded before Him. He was confident that that plan would lead Him on to greater and ever greater works, until the world should marvel at the splendor of the results -- rising from Gethsemane and Calvary through the broken grave, to the Ascension Mount and the glory of His second Advent. Oh, mystery of humiliation, that He who planned all things should will to live a life of such absolute dependence! And, yet, if He lived such a life, how much more will it become us; how much anxiety it will save us; and to what lengths of usefulness and heights of glory will it bring us! Would that we were content to wait for God to unveil His plan, so that our life might be simply the working out of His thought, the exemplification of His ideal! Let this be the cry of our hearts, "Show me thy ways, O Lord; teach me thy paths! (Psa_21:4); "teach me to do thy will" (Psa_143:10); "unto thee, O Lord, do I lift up my soul" (Psa_25:1).

God's Plans Demand Implicit Obedience

"So he arose and went to Zarephath," as before he had gone to Cherith, and as presently he would go to show himself to Ahab. A Christian lady, who had attended our services and who had learned the blessedness of a surrendered life, was soon after obliged to find another home across the ocean. She came back recently, over thousands of miles of land and sea, to visit the scene of the lesson in the hope that she would regain her former joy. But to her disappointment, though she worshiped on the same sacred spot and listened to the sounds of the well-known voice, she could not recover her joy.

At last the cause appeared. She had been living in conscious disobedience to the will of Christ, expressed through her conscience and His Word. The motives that prompted the disobedience had a touch of nobility about them but it was still disobedience, and it wrought its own penalty.

This is the true cause of failure in so many Christian lives. We catch sight of God's ideal, and become enamored with it, and we vow to be only His. We use the most emphatic words. We dedicate ourselves upon the altar. For a while we seem to tread another world, bathed in heavenly light. Then there comes a command clear and unmistakable. We must leave some beloved Cherith and go to some unwelcome Zarephath. We must speak some word, take some step, cut off some habit; and we shrink from it -- the cost is too great. But as we refuse to be obedient, the light dies off the landscape of our lives and dark clouds fling their shadows far and near.

We do not win salvation by our obedience. Salvation is the gift of God which is received by faith in the finished work of Jesus Christ our Lord. But, in being saved, we must obey. Our Savior adjures us, by the love we bear to Himself, to keep His commandments. And He does so because He wants us to taste His rarest gifts, and because He knows that in the keeping of His commandments there is great reward.

Search the Bible from board to board and see if strict, implicit, and instant obedience has not been the secret of the noblest lives that ever lit up the dull monotony of the world. The proudest title of our King was the Servant of Jehovah. And none of us can seek to realize a nobler aim than that which was the inspiration of His heart: "I come... to do thy will, O God" (Heb_10:7). Mary, the simple-hearted mother, uttered a word which is pertinent to every age, when, at the marriage feast, she turned to the servants and said, "Whatsoever he saith unto you, do it" (Joh_2:5).

Implicit Obedience Sometimes Brings Us into a Smelting Furnace

"Zarephath" means a smelting furnace. It lay outside the Land of Canaan, occupying the site of the modern Surafend which stands on a long ridge, backed by the snow-clad steeps of Hermon and overlooking the blue waters of the Mediterranean. Many things might have made it distasteful to the prophet. It belonged to the land from which Jezebel had brought her impious tribe. It was as much cursed by the terrible drought as Canaan. It was impossible to reach it save by a weary journey of one hundred miles through the heart of the land where his name was execrated, his person proscribed. And then to be sustained by a widow woman belonging to a heathen people! He would not have so much minded to have sustained her, but it was not pleasant to feel that he must be dependent on her slender earnings or meager store. Surely it was a smelting furnace for cleansing out any alloy of pride or self-reliance or independence which might be lurking in the recesses of his heart.

And there was much of the refining fire in the character of his reception. When he reached the straggling town it was probably toward nightfall. At the city gate a widow woman was gathering a few sticks to prepare the evening meal. To some it might have seemed a coincidence, but there is no such word in faith's vocabulary. That which to human judgment is a coincidence, to faith is a Providence. This was evidently the widow of whom God had spoken. Faint with thirst and weary with long travel, but never doubting that his needs would be amply met, he asked her to fetch a little water in a vessel, that he might drink. The widow may have had some premonition of his coming. There would seem to be some suggestion of this having been so, in the words, "I have commanded a widow woman there to sustain thee" (1Ki_17:9). Her Character will come out in due course; but there must have been something in her which could not be found in the many widows of the land of Israel (Luk_4:25-26). It was for no arbitrary reason that God passed them over, and went so far afield. She must have possessed qualities of Character, germs of better things, sparks of heroism and faith which distinguished her from all her sorrowing sisterhood and made her the befitting hostess of the prophet; the glad sharer with him in his Father's bounty. To her the impression was probably given of the coming of the prophet -- just as the visions to Saul and to Ananias, to Cornelius and to Peter, flashed upon them in duplicates.

She was not. therefore, surprised at the prophet's request, and silently went to fetch a small jar of water. Encouraged by her willingness, Elijah asked her to bring a morsel of bread. It was a modest request, but it unlocked the silent agony of her soul. She had no cake, but just a handful of meal in a barrel and a little oil in a cruse. She was about to make one last repast for herself and her son, who was probably too weak through long privation to be with her. Having eaten it, they had no alternative but to lie down together and die. It was very depressing for the man of God, after his long and weary march.

It is thus that God leads His people still. "And that abideth not the fire ye shall make go through the water" (Num_31:23). He will not suffer us to be tempted beyond that which we are able to bear. He will not thresh vetches with a sharp threshing instrument nor turn a cartwheel about on cummin. But it is written, "Every thing that may abide the fire, ye shall make it go through the fire, and it shall be clean" (Num_31:23). If then, there is something in you that can bear the ordeal, be sure you will be put into the furnace. But the fire shall not destroy, it shall only cleanse you. You will be put into it by the hand of love and kept in it only until patience has done her perfect work. The flames shall only consume the bonds that bind you and, as you walk loose in the fire, bystanders shall descry at your side the form of one like unto the Son of God.

When God Puts His People into the Furnace, He Will Supply All Their Needs

Circumstances were certainly very depressing, but what are they to a man whose inner self is occupied with the presence and power of God? God had said that he should be fed, and by that widow. So it should be, though the earth and heaven should pass away. Difficulties are to faith what gymnastic apparatus are to bays; means of strengthening the muscular fiber. Like the fabled salamander, faith feeds on fire. And so with heroic faith, Elijah said, "Fear not; go and do as thou hast said: ...for thus saith the LORD God of Israel, The barrel of meal shall not waste, neither shall the cruse of oil fail, until the day that the LORD sendeth rain upon the earth"" (1Ki_17:13-14).

Our only need is to inquire if we are at that point in God's pattern where He would have us be. If we are, though it seem impossible for us to be maintained, the thing impossible shall be done. We shall be sustained by a miracle if no ordinary means will suffice. "Seek ye first the kingdom of God, and his righteousness; and all these things shall be added unto you" (Mat_6:33). We reserve for future thought that unfailing meal and oil, but, before we close, we remark with what different meaning different people may use the same holy words. The widow said, as Elijah had done, "The LORD God liveth" (1Ki_17:12). But to her those words brought no comfort, because they were repeated from hearsay and not from a living experience of their truth. God forbid that they should be a parrot-speech upon our lips. But, rather, may they be burned into our inmost being -- so that we may go through life fearless of all save sin, and cheering timid hearts with the assurance of an unfaltering courage. "Fear not!" (v.13).

Chapter Four - The Spirit and Power of Elijah

How can those who have traveled in Switzerland forget the early mornings when they have been summoned from sleep to await the dawn? A weird and mysterious hush possesses nature as a crowd is hushed in expectancy of a king's approach. Then a strange light spreads outward from the eastern sky. At last one of the loftiest Alps is smitten with the roseate flush of dawn; then another, and another, and yet another, until all the peaks, mantled with untrodden snow, are lit up and transfigured with burning splendor. But during all this time the valleys below are swathed in mist and veiled in darkness. It is only after hours have passed away and the monarch of the day has climbed slowly toward his throne that the blessed sunlight penetrates to the tiny hamlets and scattered chalets, or sparkles in the brooks, or casts shadows from the stones and flowers.

This illustration will show the difference between the dispensation which closed with the first advent of our Lord and that in which it is our happiness to live, and which is to close with His glorious Epiphany. Each has been blessed with the ministry of the Holy Ghost; but it is in this age alone, dating from the day of Pentecost, that He has been poured forth on sons and daughters, and on servants and handmaidens (Act_2:17-18). Now every believer, even the humblest and the weakest, may be bathed in His divine and sacred influence; but in Elijah's time, only the elite of the household of faith knew what His eternal fullness meant. "Holy men of God spake as they were moved by the Holy Ghost" (2Pe_1:21). "The prophets... searched... what the Spirit of Christ which was in them did signify" (1Pe_1:11). The Holy Ghost was not yet given; because that Jesus was not yet glorified" (Joh_7:39).

Elijah was one of these men who were filled with the Holy Ghost. This was the Universal testimony of those who knew him best. Elisha's one desire was that he should be heir to the Spirit which was so manifestly upon his master (2Ki_2:9). "The spirit of Elijah" was a familiar phrase on the lips of the sons of the prophets (2Ki_2:15). And years after, when the angel of God spake to Zacharias in the Temple, he could find no better illustration of the presence of the Holy Ghost in his promised child, than by saying, "He shall go before Him in the spirit and power of Elias" (Luk_1:15-17).

The glorious ministry of Elijah was due not to any inherent qualities in himself but to the extraordinary indwelling of the Holy Ghost who was given to him as to other holy men of God in the old time -- through faith. If, then, we could but have that same Spirit in an equal measure, we should be able to repeat his marvelous deeds. It is said that it would be possible to gather up the mighty force of Niagara and, transforming it into electricity, carry it along a wire to drive machinery one hundred miles away. If this should ever be done, it would be a matter of almost perfect indifference whether the wire were slender or thick. The mighty force could as well travel along the slender thread, and as well perform its marvels, as through an electric cable. So the question for us all is whether the Holy Ghost is working with and through us in power. If He is, then, though our nature be paltry and weak, He shall effect through us the same mighty deeds as through men vastly our superiors in mental and moral force. Nay, we may even glory in our infirmities, that this divine power may rest upon us more conspicuously, and that the glory may be more evidently God's.

Now the question arises. May we, ordinary Christian people living in our modern society, hope to receive the Holy Spirit in that extraordinary and special measure in which He rested upon Elijah? Of course we have all received the Holy Spirit to a certain extent, or we could never have come to Jesus. All the graces of the Christian character, all our comfort, all our overcomings, are due to His presence.

Every virtue we possess,
And every victory won,
And every thought of holiness,
Are His alone.

(Author Unknown)

And yet it is clear that over and beyond this ordinary grace, which all believers must have, there is a blessed anointing of the Holy Ghost which gives special equipment and fitness for service. Elijah had it. Our blessed Lord, as the perfect servant, had it. Being full of the Holy Ghost, He returned in the power of the Spirit into Galilee, and traced His marvelous power to the fact that the Holy Spirit was upon Him (Luk_4:1; Luk_4:14; Luk_4:18). The apostles had it from the day of Pentecost when they received the fullness of the Spirit for witness- bearing, although they must have possessed Him before for personal character (compare Act_1:8;

Act_2:4 with Joh_20:22). The Samaritan believers had it, but only after Peter and John had prayed for them "that they might receive the Holy Ghost" -- although it is evident that their previous conversion and joy had been due to His blessed work (Act_8:15-16). The disciples at Ephesus had it, but only after Paul had laid his hands upon them.

This is surely what we want. And this is what we may have. This special anointing for service is not only for men like Elijah or Paul or Peter who soar far beyond us into the azure skies, but for us all as long as there stands upon the page of revelation these priceless words, "The promise [referring obviously to Act_1:4] is unto you, and to your children, and to all that are afar off, even as many as the Lord our God shall call" (Act_2:39). We are among the far-off ones, and therefore we may claim the promise for ourselves and receive the fullness of the Holy Ghost to equip us for our life and ministry.

But there are three conditions with which we must comply if we would receive and keep this blessed gift.

We Must Be Emptied

God cannot fill us if we are already filled. It took ten days to drain the apostles, even though they had spent three years under the immediate tuition of Christ. But the emptying process was an indispensable preliminary to the day of Pentecost. For Elijah, this process went on beside the drying brook and during the long and dreary march to Zarephath and throughout his sojourn there. It apparently took three years and six months. It was a long and weary waiting time, but it was well spent. As he became emptied of self, self-sufficiency, and self-dependence he became more and more filled with the Spirit of power so that Carmel itself, with all its heroic deeds, was gloriously possible to him.

Are we willing to pay this price? Are we prepared for God to empty us of all that is in the anywise contrary to his will? Are we content to be empty and broken vessels, that the river, in whose bed we lie, may easily flow through us? If not, let us ask Him to work in us to will His own good pleasure -- plunging the cold, stubborn iron into the glowing furnace of His grace until it can be bent into perfect conformity to His own glorious will. But if we are willing, let us present our emptied nature to the Son of God, that He may fill us with the fullness of the Spirit. Let us also believe that He does fill us, as soon as we yield ourselves to Him. You do not want more of Him more urgently than He wants more of you, and the one is the condition of the other (Jas_4:5 RV). Grace, like nature, abhors a vacuum. Just as the cold, fresh air will rush in to fill an exhausted receiver as soon as it has a chance to enter, so does the grace of the Holy Spirit enter the heart that can boast of nothing but an aching void. There may be no ecstasy, no rushing wind, no fiery baptism; but nevertheless, "the Lord, whom ye seek, shall suddenly come to his Temple" (Mal_3:1) in floods of silent and golden light. "Thus saith the LORD, Make this valley full of ditches. For thus saith the LORD, Ye shall not see wind, neither shall ye see rain; yet that valley shall be filled with water" (2Ki_3:16-17).

Many Christians, seeking this blessed fullness, make the same mistake as is constantly made by those who seek after forgiveness and acceptance with God. They look within for evidences of the indwelling of the Spirit and refuse to believe in His presence unless they detect certain signs which they consider befitting. This is entirely wrong. The reckoning is not of feeling but of faith.

If we have complied with God's directions we must believe, whether we feel any difference or not, that God has done His part and has kept His promise, given to us through Jesus Christ our Lord; and that He has not been slower to give us the Holy Spirit than earthly fathers are to give bread to their hungry children (Luk_11:13). When we leave the chamber where we have solemnly dedicated ourselves to God and sought to be filled with the Spirit, we must not examine our feelings to discover whether there is such a difference in us as we might expect; but we must cry in the assurance of faith, "I praise Thee, Blessed One, that Thou hast not failed to perform Thy chosen work. Thou hast entered my longing heart, and hast taken up Thine abode in me. Henceforth Thou shalt have Thy way with me, to will and do Thine own good pleasure."

We should not seek to know the presence of the Holy Ghost by any signs pointing to Himself. He reveals not Himself, but Christ. The Holy Spirit glorifies Christ (Joh_16:14). And the surest symptoms that He is within are sensitivity to sin, tenderness of conscience, and the growing love for Jesus, the fragrance of His name, sympathy with His purposes. Have you these in growing measure? Then you know somewhat of His gracious filling.

A little child was once asked her age; and she replied, "I don't feel like seven. I feel like six; but Mother says I'm seven." Here was the reckoning of faith, putting her mother's word before her own feeling. And thus we must refuse to consider ourselves, to diagnose our symptoms, or feel our pulse; but must launch out upon the deep of God's truthfulness and let down our nets for a draught of power and blessing.

We Must Be Obedient

We have already insisted on this, but it is so indispensable that repeated emphasis must be laid upon it. Christ reiterated His appeals for the keeping of His commands in almost every sentence of His closing discourses with His disciples (Joh_14:15; Joh_14:21; Joh_14:23-24). He gives the secret of His own abiding in His Father's love in these striking words: "If ye keep my commandments, ye shall abide in my love; even as I have kept my Father's commandments, and abide in his love" (Joh_15:10). Instant and implicit obedience to the teaching of the Word and the inner promptings of the Holy Spirit is an absolute condition of keeping, or increasing, the store of sacred influence. On the contrary, one little item of disobedience persisted in is quite sufficient to check all further bestowments, and even to deprive us of what we have. "If ye be willing and obedient, ye shall eat the good of the land; But if ye refuse and rebel, ye shall be devoured with the sword" (Isa_1:19-20). Nor is such obedience hard, for all God's commands are enablings, and His grace is sufficient. Look out for it. If only every believer who reads these lines would resolve from this hour to imitate Elijah, who went and did according to the word of the Lord (1Ki_17:5; 1Ki_17:8-10) -- not with the thought of merit, but beneath the inspiration of love; not in the weightier matters only, but in the crossings of the T's and in the dottings of the I's -- they would find at once that there would open before them a life of almost inconceivable glory. It is from the heights of unwavering obedience that we catch sight of the wide and open sea of blessedness. The exact obedience of Elias is the inviolable condition of receiving and keeping the spirit and power of Elijah.

We Must Live on The Word of God

Elijah, the widow, and her son lived on their daily replenished stores; but the prophet had other meat to eat which they knew not of: "Man shall not live by bread alone, but by every word that proceedeth out of the mouth of God" (Mat_4:4). It was on that word that Elijah fed during those long and slow- moving days. Sometimes he would climb up the heights behind the little town, in deep meditation upon that Word which is like the great mountains. Sometimes he would pace the seashore, musing on those judgments which are a great deep. He could say, "Thy words were found, and I did eat them; and thy word was unto me the joy and rejoicing of mine heart! (Jer_15:16). And sitting with the widow and her son, he would make that Word the topic of his constant talk; so that she was compelled to refer to it in these significant terms: "I know... that the word of the LORD in thy mouth is truth" (1Ki_17:24).

26

This is the further absolute condition of becoming and remaining filled with the Holy Ghost. The Spirit works with and through the Word. What the metal is to the locomotive, what the wire is to the electric spark, what the grammar is to the teacher -- the Word of God is to the Spirit of God. If we neglect the reverent study of Scripture we cut ourselves off from the very vehicle through which God's Spirit teaches human spirits. And this is the great fault of our times. Christian people will attend conventions, plunge into all kinds of Christian work, read many good books about the Bible and Christian living; but they give the Bible itself the most cursory and superficial heed. And it is for this reason that the Bible does not speak to them.

If you would know all the wondrous beauty of a forest glade, you must not be satisfied with passing through it with hasty foot and in company with a troop of merry children whose ringing laughter carries panic into the hearts of thousands of shy living things that, with trembling hearts, keep still in hole and brake and nest. No, you must go alone and sit quietly down on the log of some felled tree and wait. Then the mystery of beauty will begin to unfold itself: the fairy bowers, the mossy glens, the interlacing boughs. Presently a note will sound from yonder bough, as the signal for the outburst of many sweet-voiced choristers, and the woodland will ring with the music of the birds while the squirrel runs up some neighboring tree, and the rabbits come out to feed, and the young foxes play about their holes. All this is hidden from those who cannot wait. So there are mysteries of glory and beauty in Scripture hidden from the wise and prudent but revealed to babes. There is no book that will so repay time spent over its pages as the Word of God.

A neglected Bible means a starved and strengthless spirit, a comfortless heart, a barren life, and a grieved Holy Ghost. If the people who are now perpetually running about to meetings for crumbs of help and comfort, would only stay at home and search their Bibles, there would be more happiness in the Church and more blessing on the world. It is very prosaic counsel, but it is true.

We reserve our next chapter for an account of the life of this Spirit-filled man and the household in which he dwelt. Suffice it now to say that the Holy Ghost, which dwelt in so largely, revealed Himself in those very traits which must always be His fruits: gentleness under provocation, steadfastness in trial, power in prayer, life victorious over death. But we may note, in closing, the remarkable admission of the widow: "I know that thou art a man of God" (1Ki_17:24).

We talk of the man of letters, the man of honor, the man of mark; but how infinitely better to be known as a man of God -- one of God's men, a man after God's own heart! And how splendid the tribute when we are so addressed by those with whom we live! "Familiarity breeds contempt" is a cliche, but when a man is filled with the Holy Ghost; the more he is known, the more clearly he is proved to be a man of God.

And in Elijah's case, the power of the indwelling Spirit evinced itself in the marvelous effect produced on that widow and her child. The widow was convinced of sin and led to the truth of God. The son was brought back from death into life. And such result shall accrue in our experiences, if we will only seek to be filled with the fullness of God. "He that believeth in me, the works that I do shall he do also; and greater works than these shall he do; because I go unto my Father" (Joh_14:12). "Ye shall receive power, after that the Holy Ghost is come upon you" (Act_1:8).

Chapter Five - The Test of the Homelife

Many a man might bear himself as a hero and saint in the solitudes of Cherith, or on the heights of Carmel, and yet wretchedly fail in the homelife of Zarephath. It is one thing to commune with God in the solitudes of nature and perform splendid acts of devotion and zeal for Him in the presence of thousands, but it is quite another to walk with Him day by day in the midst of a home with its many calls for the constant forgetfulness of self. Blessed, indeed, is the homelife on whose threshold we cast aside our reserve, our attitude of self-defense, our suspicions and our fears, and resign ourselves to the unquestioning trust of those whose love puts the tenderest construction on much that the world exaggerates and distorts!

And yet it would be idle to deny that there is much to try and test us just where the flowers bloom and the voices of hate and passion die away in distant murmurs. There is a constant need for the exercise of gentleness, patience, self-sacrifice, and self-restraint. And beneath the test of homelife with its incessant duties and demands, many men break down -- even men whose characters seem far above the average.

This ought not to be, nor need it be. If our religion is what it should be, it will resemble the law of gravitation, which not only controls the planets in their spheres but guides the course of each dust grain through the autumn breeze and determines the fall of a rose petal fluttering to the path. Everything will come beneath its sway -- each look, each word, each trivial act. Indeed, we shall show the reality and thoroughness of our religion when it is no longer a garment to be put off and on at will, but when it pervades us as life does the organism in which it is contained. The truly religious man will be as sweet in irritating gnat stings as in crushing calamities, as self-denying for a child as for a crowd, as patient over a spoiled or late meal as over an operation which summons all his manhood to the front. "My grace is sufficient for thee" (2Co_12:6) is the one answer of Jesus Christ to all inquiries, the one reply to all excuses and complaints about trying circumstances.

Your homelife was chosen for you by the unerring skill of One who knows you better than you know yourself and who cannot make a mistake. It has been selected as the best school of grace for you. Its burdens were poised on the hand of infinite love, before they were placed on your shoulders. Its pressure has been carefully measured by scales more delicate than those which chemists use. And now, looking down upon you, the Master says: "There is nothing in your life that may not be lived in Me, for Me, through Me, and I am willing to enable you to be sweet, and noble, and saint-like in it all."

In the last chapter we saw something of the power and Spirit with which Elijah was filled. It was nothing less than the Holy Ghost Himself, and we learned that that same glorious gift is for each of us. Indeed, it is our bounden duty never to rest until we are filled with that same fullness and clothed in that same robe. But we are now to follow him into a home and see how he bears the test of home life, and we shall learn to admire and love him the more. He lived a truly human life. He was not too great or good for human nature's daily food.

He was the same man in the widow's house as on Carmel's heights. He is like one of those mountains to which we have referred, piercing the heavens with unscalable heights but clothed about the lower parts with woodlands, verdant fields, and smiling bowers where bees gather honey, and children play. He shows that when a man is full of the Holy Ghost, it will be evidenced by the entire tenor of his daily walk and conversation. In this he reminds us of Luther, the Elijah of modern times, who stood alone against the apostasy of the Romish church; but whose family life was a model of beauty -- an oasis in the desert. Let those who only know Luther as the Reformer read his letters to his little daughter, and they will be captivated by the winsomeness and tenderness of that great and gentle soul.

Elijah Teaches Us Contentment

The fare in the widow's home was frugal enough and there was only enough of it for their daily needs. Human nature, which was as strong in the prophet as in the rest of us, would have preferred to be able to count sacks of meal and barrels of oil. It would have been pleasant to go into some spacious storeroom and, looking around on the abundant provision, say, "I have goods enough to carry me through the years of famine. I will eat, drink, and be merry." But this is not God's way nor is it the healthiest discipline for our better life.

God's rule is, Day by day. God provides for each day as it comes. The manna fell on the desert sands each day, enough for that day. But it fell every day without fail. God will provide us with enough strength each day to meet that day's demands: "as thy days, so shall thy strength be" (Deu_33:25). And they who live like this are constantly reminded of their blessed dependence on their Father's love. They are led back again to the life of the little child. They know nothing of those temptations to self-sufficiency which work ruin in the rich as the myriads of minute insects of the southern seas silently eat away the bottoms of mighty vessels which are able to defy the storms.

If God were to give us the choice between seeing our provision and keeping it ourselves or not seeing it and leaving Him to deal it out, day by day; most of us would be almost sure to choose the former alternative. It gratifies our sense of importance to count up our stores, our barrels, and our sacks. It invests us with so much superiority to our neighbors. It gives such a sense of security. But we should be far wiser to say, "I am content to trust Thee, Father, the living God who gives us all things richly to enjoy. Keep Thou the stores under Thine own hand; they will give me less anxiety, they will not lead me into temptation, they will not expose me to be jealous of others less favored than myself."

And those who live thus are not worse off than others; nay, in the truest sense, they are better off because the responsibility of maintaining them rests wholly upon God. They are delivered from the fret of anxiety, the strain of daily care, and the temptations which make it almost impossible for a rich man to enter the kingdom of God. If God guarantees, as He does, our support, does it much matter whether we can SEE the sources from which He will obtain it? It might gratify our curiosity, but it would not make them more sure. They are in existence and beneath His eye; and they will come safely to our hand. The main thing is to understand the precious promise, "Seek ye first the kingdom of God and his righteousness, and all these things shall be added unto you" (Mat_6:33). Then let us go on doing our duty, filling our time, working out the plan of our life. We may be as free from care as the birds that have neither storehouse nor barn. We may laugh as merrily as the child who comes in from school to eat and goes out again to play and is utterly thoughtless about his next meal. We may be entirely destitute, our pantry bare, our money exhausted, and our means of livelihood gone. But our Father has ample resources. His are the cattle on a thousand hills, and His the waving corn-fields, and the myriad fish of the ocean depths. His hired servants have bread enough and to spare, He has prepared a supply for our need, and He will deliver it in time. We only need to trust Him.

It is impossible to tell whose eyes may read these words, but if they should be read by those whose aim it is to be independent, let them consider what they mean. Do they mean to be independent of God or of men? They will live to see that they can be independent of neither. And the serious question presents itself, Is this a worthy aim for those who are bought slaves of Christ? Surely we are meant to be stewards; not storing up our Lord's money for ourselves, but administering for Him all that we do not need for the maintenance of ourselves and our dear ones in the position of life in which God has placed us. And our only worldly aim should be to lay out our Lord's money to the very best advantage so that we may render Him an account with joy when He comes to reckon with us.

If, on the other hand, these words are read by those who are dependent on daily supplies -- with little hope of ever owning more than the daily handful of meal and the little oil at the bottom of the cruse -- let them be comforted by the example of Elijah. "Be content with such things as ye have; for he hath said, I will never leave thee, nor forsake thee" (Heb_13:5). The bottom of the barrel may have been scraped today; but tomorrow there will be just enough in it for tomorrow's needs. The last drop of oil may have been drained today, but there will be enough for tomorrow. Anxiety will not do you good; but the prayer of faith will. "Your Father knoweth what things ye have need of." He who lit life's flame knows how much fuel is required to keep it burning. Throw all responsibility on God. He who gave His own Son will with Him freely give all things. Do not listen to the arch-liar, who bids you distrust and despair. He has never yet been justified by the event. His prophecies have always proved false. His insinuations are simply beds of rank and poisonous stinging nettles. Do not lie down in them, but trample them beneath your feet. Oh that we might learn, though it be in the school of privation to be content in whatever state we are and to be able to cry with one of Elijah's compeers, "I can do all things through Christ which strengtheneth me" (Php_4:13). "For thus saith the LORD God of Israel, The barrel of meal shall not waste, neither shall the cruse of oil fail, until the day that the LORD sendeth rain upon the earth" (1Ki_17:14).

31

Elijah Also Teaches Us Gentleness Under Provocation

We do not know how long the mother hung over her dying child. He may have been struck down like the little fellow who cried, "My head! my head!" and faded in one summer's afternoon, or he may have lingered beneath the spell of a wearying illness which not only wore out his life but overtaxed his mother's nerves so that she spoke unadvisedly and cruelly to the man who had brought deliverance to her home. "Art thou come unto me to call my sin to remembrance, and to slay my son?" (1Ki_17:18).

A remark so uncalled for and unjust might well have stung the prophet to the quick or prompted a bitter reply. And it would doubtless have done so, had his goodness been anything less than inspired by the Holy Ghost. But one of the fruits of His indwelling is gentleness. "The fruit of the Spirit is love, joy, peace, long-suffering, gentleness" (Gal_5:22). The nature breathed into the spirit by the blessed Spirit of God is identical with His own which is love: and... "Charity [love] suffereth long, and is kind; ... is not easily provoked; ... beareth all things; believeth all things; hopeth all things; endureth all things" (1Co_13:4-7). Thus it happened that Elijah simply said, "Give me thy son" (1Ki_17:19). If there were a momentary uprising of indignation it was immediately quelled by the Dove which had come to brood in the nest of his heart.

We need more of this practical godliness. Many deceive themselves. They go to fervid meetings and profess that they have placed all upon the altar. They speak as if they were indeed filled with the Holy Ghost. But when they return to their homes, the least friction, or interference with their plans, or mistake on the part of others, or angry outburst arouses a sudden and violent manifestation of temper. Such people have not yet experienced His special grace. There is much more for them to learn. He who first led them to Jesus is able to make them meek with His meekness, and gentle with His gentleness. He can give them victory over their natural infirmities as well as over all conscious sin. He can work so great a transformation within them that "instead of the thorn shall come up the fir tree, and instead of the brier shall come up the myrtle tree; and it shall be to the LORD for a name, for an everlasting sign that shall not be cut off" (Isa_55:13).

If the Holy Spirit is really filling the heart, there will come over the rudest, the least refined, the most selfish person a marvelous change. There will be a gentleness in speech, a softness of the voice, a tender thoughtfulness in the smallest actions, an expression of abiding peace on the face. These shall be the evident seal of the Holy Ghost, the mint-mark of heaven. Are they evident in ourselves?

Gentle Spirit, dwell with me,
I myself would gentle be;
And with words that help and heal,
Would Thy life in mine reveal.

(Author Unknown)

Elijah Teaches Also the Power of a Holy Life

Somewhere in the background of this woman's life there was a dark deed which dwarfed all other memories of wrongdoing and stood out before her mind as her sin (1Ki_17:18). What it was we do not know. It may have been connected with the birth of that very son. It had probably been committed long years before and had then filled her with a keen agony of mind, for conscience is not inoperative even in the hearts of the children of idolatry and heathendom (Rom_2:14-15). But in later years, the keen sense of remorse had become dulled; conscience long outraged had grown benumbed. Sometimes she even lost all recollection of her sin for weeks and months together. We all have a wonderful faculty of dismissing from us an unwelcome thought, just as men try to hide from themselves the obvious symptoms of a disease which is sapping the forces of life.

Memory fixes all impressions and retains them. It never permits them to be destroyed, though it may not always be able to produce them instantly to a given call. Some memories are like well-classified libraries in which you can readily discover even the smallest pamphlet, while others are so confused that they are useless for practical purposes. Yet, even in these nothing that ever came within their range has ever been lost, and whenever the right clue is presented there is an immediate resurrection and recovery of sounds and sights and trains of thought long buried.

How terrible will it be when the lost soul is met on the threshold of the dark world to which it goes, by the solemn words, "Son, Remember!" And what more fearful punishment could we imagine than being compelled to meet again and confront the hideous past, summoned by an inevitable remembrancer while conscience, no longer stupefied and drugged, is sensitive enough to convince of the exceeding sinfulness of sin.

It is remarkable how different is the mental stimulus which is required by different castes of mind to awaken dormant memories. In the

33

case of some, the handwriting on an old letter, a picture, a scent borne on the breeze, or a song will be enough. Their own sorrow reminded Joseph's brethren of their disgraceful behavior to their brother thirty years before. But in the case of the woman of Zarephath it was Elijah's holy life, combined with her own terrible sorrow. Beneath the spell of these two voices her memory gave up its dead, and her conscience was quickened into vigorous life. "Art thou come unto me to call my sin to remembrance?" (1Ki_17:18).

Oh, to live in the power of the Holy Ghost! Our looks would sometimes then convict the stoutest sinners of sin, as it is recorded of Finney whose grieved face brought conviction to a young woman and through her to a whole factory of operatives. Our holy walk would be a standing rebuke, a mirror in which the sin-pocked might see the ravages wrought by sin. Our words would then be sharp two-edged swords, piercing to the dividing of the joints and marrow, of soul and spirit.

And if any shall be conscious of some hidden but unforgiven sin, let that one know that all efforts to forget will some day be unavailing. Sickness, or bereavement, or bitter loss may come. Then that sin will spring up as if only committed yesterday, in all its horror and agony. It is said that the spirit of the victim haunts the murderer until he makes reparation by confession and surrender. There is some truth in it, for sin is only blotted out of remembrance, both of God and the soul, when it has been confessed and put beneath the blood of Jesus. Confess your sin and claim that cleansing now, and you will hear the voice of God saying, "Their sins and iniquities will I remember no more" (Heb_10:17).

Elijah Teaches the Secret of Giving Life

It is a characteristic of those who are filled with the Holy Ghost, that they carry with them everywhere the spirit of life, even resurrection life. We shall not only convince men of sin, but we shall become channels through which the divine life may enter them. Thus was it with the prophet. But mark the conditions under which alone we shall be able to fulfill this glorious function.

1. LONELY WRESTLINGS.

"He took him out of her bosom, and carried him up into a loft, where he abode, and laid him upon his own bed. And he cried unto the LORD" (1Ki_17:19-20). We are not specific enough in prayer, and we do not spend enough time in intercession, dwelling with holy ardor on each beloved name and on each heartrending case. What wonder that we achieve so little!

2. HUMILITY.

"He stretched himself upon the child three times" (1Ki_17:21). How wonderful that so great a man should spend so much time and thought on that slender frame and be content to bring himself into direct contact with that which might be thought to defile! It is a touching spectacle, but we must imitate it in some measure. We must seek the conversion of children, winning them before Satan or the world attach them. But to do so, we must stoop to them; becoming as little children to win little children for Jesus.

3. PERSEVERANCE.

"He stretched himself upon the child three times, and cried unto the LORD" (1Ki_17:21). He was not soon daunted. It is thus that God tests the genuineness of our desire. These deferred answers lead us to lengths of holy boldness and pertinacity of which we should not otherwise have dreamed, but from which we shall never go back. "Men ought always to pray, and not to faint! (Luk_18:1).

And his supplication met with the favor of God. "The LORD heard the voice of Elijah; and the soul of the child came into him again, and he revived" (1Ki_17:22). And as the prophet presented him to the grateful and rejoicing mother, he must have been beyond all things gratified with her simple testimony to the reality and power of the life which the Holy Ghost had begotten within him: "Now by this I know that thou art a man of God, and that the word of the LORD in thy mouth is truth" (1Ki_17:24). And what was the result of all?

Her work was small, her conceptions obscure, her home Gentile and heathen. Yet, because her motives were noble and her spirit in sympathy with Elijah's, it was announced by Him, at whose throne we must all stand for our reward, that she had done what she could, and her crown should shine as brightly as that placed on the brow of the prophet of God. We are rewarded, not according to our sphere or the results of our work, but according to the sincerity and beauty of our motives. These may be as lofty in an obscure widow as in Elijah himself.

Chapter Six - Obadiah -- A Contrast

After many days the word of the Lord again summoned Elijah to be on the move. Months, and even years had passed in the retirement of Zarephath. The widow and her son had become bound to him by the most sacred ties. The humble home, with its loft and barrel of meal and cruse of oil, was hallowed with the delightful memories of the unfailing carefulness of God.

It must have been a great trial for him to go, and how great was the contrast that awaited him! He had probably heard of Ahab's search for him through all the neighboring countries. There was not a nation or kingdom where the incensed monarch had not sent to seek him, demanding an oath from the rulers that he was not in hiding there. It was not likely, therefore, that he would be received with much courtesy. Nay, the probability was that he would be instantly arrested and perhaps put to torture to extort a revocation of the words which had placed the realm under the terrible interdict of drought. And as he contrasted the tumultuous roar of the waves foaming outside the harbor with he calm peace that reigned in the haven of rest which had sheltered him so long, he might well have shrunk back in dismay. But he had no alternative but to go. He who had said, "Go hide thyself," now said, "Go show thyself" (1Ki_18:1). What was he but a servant, bound to obey? And so, with the implicit obedience which has arrested our attention more than once, "Elijah went to show himself unto Ahab" (1Ki_18:2).

In this new departure the prophet evidently encouraged himself by the words on which he had leaned when first he entered the monarch's presence, "The LORD of hosts liveth, before whom I stand" (1Ki_18:15). And there may have rung through his spirit a refrain, throbbing with heroic faith, uttered centuries before by a kindred soul: "The LORD is my light and my salvation; whom shall I fear? the LORD is the strength of my life; of whom shall I be afraid? When the wicked, even mine enemies and my foes, came upon me to eat up my flesh, hey stumbled and fell. Though an host should encamp against me, my heart shall not fear: though war should rise against me, in this will I be confident" (Psa_27:1-3).

But, though Elijah's spirit was thus fortified against fear, it must have been very bitter to him to see the devastation which had been wrought in the land. The music of the brooklets was still. No green pastures carpeted the hills or vales. There was neither blossom on the fig tree nor fruit in the vines; and the labor of the olive failed. The ground was chapped and barren. The hinds calved in the field and deserted their young because there was no grass. The wild asses, with distended nostrils, climbed the hills to snuff up the least breath of air that might allay the fever of their thirst. And, probably, the roads in the neighborhood of the villages and towns were dotted by the stiffened corpses of the abject poor who had succumbed to the severity of their privations. We have no idea, in these temperate regions, of the horrors of an Eastern drought. All this had been brought about instrumentally by the prophet's prayer, and it would have been intolerable, had he not eagerly hoped that his people would learn the exceeding sinfulness and evil of sin. "Thine own wickedness shall correct thee, and thy backslidings shall reprove thee: know therefore, and see, that it is an evil thing and bitter, that thou hast forsaken the Lord thy God" (Jer_2:19).

Though the famine was sore everywhere, it seems to have been most severe in Samaria. "There was a sore famine in Samaria." And it was this famine that brought out the true character of Ahab. We might have supposed that he would set himself to alleviate the miseries of his people; and, above all, that he would have turned back to God; but no -- his one thought was about the horses and mules of his stud; and his only care was to save some of them alive. And so he starts on a mission -- such as is still undertaken by the petty chieftains of Eastern tribes -- to find grass. What selfishness is here! Mules and asses before his people! Seeking for grass instead of seeking for God!

And yet such selfishness is as rife today as ever. Selfishness like this prompts the great ones of the earth to dash myriads of men against each other in the shock of battle, for the gratification of a mere personal pique, and regardless of the untold misery inflicted on thousands of hearts and homes. Selfishness like this makes men of wealth and fashion loll on beds of down, roll in luxurious carriages, and feast sumptuously every day -- indifferent to the hopeless wretchedness of those who earn their wealth and are paid a starvation wage. Selfishness like this still spends on an equipage, a horse, a dog, the keeping of a shooting-box, the round of amusements, more than it can afford for the maintenance of God's work or for the relief of the poor. Are professing Christians clear in this matter? Are there not many who spend as much on a single dinner party as they do on the needs of a dying world? And what is this but a repetition of the sin of Ahab, who went out to find grass for his beasts, while his people were left to take their chance! Oh, that this spirit of selfishness were exorcised by the Spirit of Christ! Then missionary societies would not be hampered in their operations for want of funds; then the coffers of charitable institutions would be filled; then many a hard working toiler would be able to give effect to schemes now blighted and arrested by the east wind of want. I do not blame Christian men for maintaining themselves in that position of life in which they were called. It is their apparent duty to retain that position as a sacred talent (1Co_7:20; 1Co_7:24). But I cannot understand a man daring to call himself a Christian and spending more upon the accessories and luxuries of his life than he does upon that service of man which is so dear to our Lord. This is surely the selfishness of Ahab.

It is startling to find such a man as Obadiah occupying so influential position at Ahab's court. "Obadiah was the governor (or steward) of his house" (1Ki_18:3). Now, according to his own testimony, Obadiah had feared the Lord from his youth (1Ki_18:12). This is also the testimony of the sacred historian concerning him: "Obadiah feared the LORD greatly" (v.3). And he had given conspicuous proof of his piety. When Jezebel had swept the land with the besom of persecution, hunting down the prophets of the Lord and consigning them to indiscriminate slaughter, he had rescued a hundred of the proscribed men, hiding them by fifty in a cave and feeding them with bread and water. But though a good man, there was evidently a great lack of moral strength in his character. Otherwise he could never have held the position he did in the court of Ahab and Jezebel.

There is no possible harm in a Christian man holding a position of influence in a court or society where he can do so at no cost of principle. On the contrary, it may enable him to render priceless service to the cause of God. Where would Luther and the Reformation have been, humanly speaking, had it not been for the Elector of Saxony? And what would have been the fate of our Wycliffe, if John o'Gaunt had not constituted him his ward? But very few can occupy such a position without putting kid on their hands and velvet on their lips, without dropping something of their uncompromising speech, or dipping their colors to the flag of expediency. And there is every indication that this was the weak point with Obadiah.

Obadiah did not believe in carrying matters too far. Of course he could not fall in with this new order of things, but then there was no need for him to force his religious notions on everyone. He was often shocked at what he saw at court and found it hard to keep still, but then it was no business of his, and it would not do to throw up his situation, for he would be sure to lose it if he spoke out. He was often sad at heart to witness the sufferings of the prophets of the Lord and almost inclined to take up their cause, but then a single man could not do much. Perhaps he could help them better in a quiet way by keeping where he was, though it might sometimes be a little strain on his principles. The poor man must often have been in a great strait to reconcile his duty to Jehovah with his duty to his other master, Ahab. And Elijah shrewdly hinted at it, when he said, "Go, tell thy lord, Behold, Elijah is here!" Imagine a courtier of Oliver Cromwell trying to be true to the Commonwealth and to the cause of the exiled Stuarts! The life of policy and expediency is like ropewalking -- it needs considerable practice in the art of balancing.

There are scores of Obadiahs everywhere in the professing church. They know the right, and are secretly trying to do it; but they say as little about religion as they can. They never rebuke sin. They never confess their true colors. They find pretexts and excuses to satisfy the remonstrances of an uneasy conscience. They are as nervous of being identified by declared Christians as Obadiah was of being identified as a follower of Jehovah when Elijah sent him to Ahab. They are sorry for those who suffer persecution for righteousness' sake, but it never occurs to them to stand in the pillory by their side. They content themselves with administering some little relief to them, as Obadiah did to the harried prophets, but as they conceal that relief from the world, they put it in as a claim to the people of God for recognition and protection, as Obadiah did. "Was it not told my lord what I did?" (1Ki_18:13). They sometimes are on the point of throwing up all to take up an uncompromising attitude, but they find it hard to go forth to suffer affliction with the people of God as long as they are well provided for within the palace walls.

What a contrast between Obadiah and Elijah! And it is with the purpose of accentuating that contrast and of bringing out into fuller relief the noble character of the prophet, that we have sought to elaborate this sketch of Ahab's steward.

There Is a Contrast Between the Inside and The Outside of the Camp For Witnessing

There is much said on both sides of the case. Many amongst us advise that the children of God should stay in the camp of the world -- joining in its festivities, going to its places of amusements, taking the lead in its fashion and its course. In this way they hope to temper and steady it, to level it up, to make it Christian. It is a fair dream, exceedingly congenial to our natural tastes. If it were only true, it would save a world of trouble. The poor prophets of the Lord might come back from their caves, Elijah might become Ahab's vizier, and Obadiah's conscience might settle to rest. Indeed, Elijah's policy would be a supreme mistake, and we had better all become Obadiahs at once.

But there are two insurmountable difficulties in the way of our accepting this theory of leveling up from within.

1. IT IS IN DIRECT OPPOSITION TO THE TEACHING OF SCRIPTURE.

Come out from her, my people, is the one summons than rings like a clarion note from board to board. "Come out from among them, and be ye separate, saith the Lord; and touch not the unclean thing" (2Co_6:17). There is not a single hero or saint whose name sparkles on the inspired page who moved his times from within. All, without exception, have raised the cry, "Let us go forth without the camp;" and have joined the constant stream of martyrs, confessors, prophets, and saints, of whom the world is not worthy, but who can trace their kinship to Him of whom it is written, "He suffered without the gate." The only Scriptural course for God's witnesses is to go out to Him without the camp; in the world, but not of it; wearing the pilgrim garb, manifesting the pilgrim spirit, uttering the pilgrim confession.

2. THIS THEORY WILL NOT WORK.

The Man who goes into the world to level it up will soon find himself leveled down. Was not this the case with Obadiah? Instead of getting Ahab to think with himself, Ahab sent him to all fountains of water and to all brooks to find grass for his horses and mules. Surely this was a miserable errand for one who feared the Lord greatly! But this is only a sample of the kind of things which must be borne and done by such as try to serve two masters. Compare the influence exerted on the behalf of Sodom by Abraham on the heights of Mamre, with that of Lot, who, not content with pitching his tent toward the city gate, went to live inside and even became one of the judges in the city (Gen_19:1). Remember that Lot was carried captive in the sack of Sodom; but Abraham rescued him. But why need we multiply instances? This matter is undergoing daily proof. The Christian woman who marries an ungodly man is in imminent danger of being soon dragged down to his level. The servant of God who enters into partnership with a man of the world cannot keep the business from drifting. The church which admits the world into its circle will find that it will get worldly quicker than the world will become Christian.

The safest and strongest position is outside the camp. Archimedes said that he could move the world, if only he had a point of rest given him outside it. Thus, too, can a handful of God's servants influence their times, if only they resemble Elijah, whose life was spent altogether outside the pale of the court and the world of his time.

There is A Contrast Between Preventive and Aggressive Goodness

Obadiah sought simply to prevent a great harm being done. He shielded the prophets from the sword of Jezebel and the touch of famine. And this was well. Preventive goodness like this serves a very useful purpose.

It rears homes and refuges and bulwarks of defense behind which persecuted and threatened lives may thrive. But after all, the world needs something more. It is not enough to deal with the poisoned streams, a hand is needed to cast the healing salt into the fountainhead. There is an urgent demand for men like Elijah and John the Baptist who dare oppose the perpetrators of evil deeds and arraign them before the bar of God and compel them to bow before the offended majesty of a broken law.

For this there is needed a positive enduement of power which cannot be had by the half-hearted but is the glad prerogative of those who, from the crown of the head to the sole of the foot, are servants of God. Obadiah had no power of this kind. How could he have? On the other hand, Elijah was full of it. Because he was so, he succeeded in arresting the tides of sin when they were in full flood.

It is not enough to shelter the prophets, we must go and show ourselves to Ahab. We may be as sugar, but we must also be like salt that stays the progress of consumption. The preventive and ameliorative, the healing agency, is good; but the aggressive is better still, because it deals with the hidden causes of things. May God send to His Church a handful of lion-like men, like Elijah, of whom this is the majestic record: "Elijah went to show himself unto Ahab" (1Ki_18:2) to confront the royal culprit, to lay the king under arrest.

There Is a Contrast Between the Caution of Expediency and the Fearlessness of Faith

When Elijah told Obadiah to tell his master that Elijah was waiting for Ahab, the astonished courtier was incredulous. He knew how irritated and incensed Ahab had been, and that his anger was at white heat still. It seemed madness for the prophet to expose himself to its flames. Indeed, he thought either that the prophet did not know the way in which the king had sought for him or that the Spirit of the Lord would carry him off before they could meet. It never occurred to him that Elijah dare meet the king if he really know how matters stood. And even supposing that Obadiah himself were foolhardy enough to confront the king, surely God would prevent him from stepping into the lion's lair. In any case, Obadiah wished to have nothing to do with it. He was more anxious for himself than for the work of God or the wishes of Elijah. Twice over he repeated the words, "He shall slay me" (1Ki_18:9; 1Ki_18:12). And it was only when Elijah appealed to God as the witness of his solemn oath and assured Obadiah that he would surely show himself to Ahab before the sun went down that he reluctantly went to meet Ahab and told him. How unable he was to form a true conception of the fearlessness of Elijah!

And what was the source of that fearlessness? Surely it is unfolded to us in the words of Elijah's sublime asseveration: "As the LORD of hosts liveth, before whom I stand" (2Ki_3:14). God was more real to Elijah than Ahab. He was a courtier in the throne room of the King of kings. How could he be afraid of a man that should die, and of the son of man that should become as the grass of the mower's scythe withered by the noontide heat? The fear of God had made him impervious to all other fear. Faith sees the mountain full of horses and chariots of fire. Faith can hear the tread of twelve legions of angels marshaling for its defense. Faith can detect the outlines of those Almighty hands which hide the children of God in their hollow. And so, with unblanched face and undismayed heart, God's Elijahs go on to do His commands, though their way is blocked by as many devils as there are tiles upon the housetops. The Obadiahs assert that they will never dare to carry their proposals through, but they live to see their predictions falsified and their mean suggestions shamed.

There Is a Contrast Between the Reception Given to These Two Types of Character by The Ungodly

Ahab could tolerate Obadiah, because he never rebuked him. When salt has lost its savor it does not sting, though it be rubbed into an open wound. But as soon as Ahab saw Elijah, he accosted him as the great troubler of the time. "It came to pass, when Ahab saw Elijah, that Ahab said unto him, Is it thou, thou troubler of Israel?" (1Ki_18:17 RV). Years after, speaking of another devoted servant of God, whose advice was demanded by Jehoshaphat, this same Ahab said, "I hate him; for he doth not prophesy good concerning me, but evil" (1Ki_22:8).

There is no higher testimony to the consistency of our life than the hearty hatred of the Ahabs around us. One of the most scathing condemnations that could be pronounced on men is contained in those terrible words of our Lord: "The world cannot hate you; but me it hateth, because I testify of it, that the works thereof are evil" (Joh_7:7). Who would not undergo all the hate that the Ahabs can heap on us rather than incur that sentence from the lips of Christ! "Blessed are ye, when men shall revile you, and persecute you, and shall say all manner of evil against you falsely, for my sake. Rejoice, and be exceeding glad (Mat_5:11-12). If all men speak well of you, you may begin to question whether you are not becoming mere Obadiahs. But if Ahab accuses you of troubling him, rejoice;

and tell him to his face that his trouble is due to a broken commandment, and to the idols before which he bows. If there should read these lines those who are in trouble, enduring affliction, their life smitten with drought, let them ask whether the cause is not to be found in broken vows, in desecrated temples, in forfeited oaths. If so, return at once, with tears of penitence and words of confession, unto the Lord. "He hath torn, and he will heal us; he hath smitten, and he will bind us up" (Hos_6:1).

There, face to face, we leave Ahab and Elijah. We need not ask which is the more royal of the two, nor need we spend our time in looking for Obadiah. We cannot but admire the noble bearing of the prophet of God. But let us remember it was due, not to his inherent character, but to his faith. By faith he quenched the violence of fire, escaped the edge of the sword, out of weakness was made strong, stopped the mouth of this lion. And if we will acquire a similar faith, we may anticipate similar results on the meaner platform of our own lives.

Chapter Seven - The Plan of Campaign

When Elijah left Zarephath, his mind was utterly destitute of any fixed plan of action. He knew that he must show himself to Ahab and than rain was not far away, for these were his definite marching orders: "Go, show thyself unto Ahab; and I will send rain upon the earth" (1Ki_18:1). But more than that he knew not. There may have flitted before his spirit dim previsions of that sublime conflict on Carmel's heights, but he knew nothing certainly. His one endeavor was to quiet his eager nature like a weaned child, hushing it with the lullaby of an old refrain: "My soul, wait thou only upon God, for my expectation is from Him" (Psa_62:5).

The plan of this great campaign for God's truth against Baal's falsehood may have been revealed to Elijah on his journey from Zarephath to find Ahab. It may have been a sudden glance as when a lightning-flash reveals to be a benighted traveler the winding pathway he must follow through the vale beneath. But it is quite as likely that it was revealed in pieces, like those of a children's puzzle -- handed out one by one from the parent to the child, who might be confused with more than one at a time. This is so often God's way, and they who trust Him utterly are quite pleased to have it so. There is even a novelty and beauty in life when every step is unforeseen and unexpected and opens up new vistas of loveliness in God's management and in Himself.

If we seek to think ourselves into Elijah's attitude of heart and mind as he left the shelter of Zarephath and began to pass through the incidents that culminated in Carmel, it seems to have been threefold. And surely it is of surpassing interest to learn how such a man felt as he approached the sublime crisis of his life.

He Was Filled with A Consuming Passion for The Glory of God

"Let it be known that Thou are God in Israel." This prayer is the key to his heart. He neither knew nor cared to know what would become of himself; but his soul was on fire with a holy jealousy for the glory of God. He could not bear to think of those wrecked altars or martyred prophets. He could not bear to think how the Land of Promise was groaning beneath the obscene and deadly rites of Phoenician idolatry. He could not bear to think that his people were beginning to imagine that the God of Abraham, Isaac, and Israel had abdicated in favor of these false deities which were newly brought in. And when he was compelled to face these things, his spirit was stirred to its depths with indignation and sorrow.

Well would it be if each one of us was similarly inspired! We are very eager for the success of our work, our church, our sect. If these thrive, we are satisfied. If these languish, we are depressed. We are wholly occupied with the interests of our own tiny pools, oblivious of the great sea of divine glory lying nearby in perpetual sunshine. Is it wonderful that we have so small a measure of success? God will not give His glory to another, nor His praise to the graven images of our own conceit. But in this, also, God is willing to life our daily experience to the level of our loftiest ideals. Only trust Him to do it. Ask and expect Him to fill you with the fire of that zeal which burned in the heart of Elijah, consuming all that was base, corrupt, and selfish; making the whole man a fit agent for God. This was no indigenous growth. It was not more natural to him than it is to any one of us. It was simply one of the fruits of the indwelling of the Holy Ghost, who is equally promised to the most ignoble nature.

He Was Profoundly Convinced That He Was Only a Servant

"Let it be known that thou are God in Israel; and that I am thy servant." It was not for the slave in olden times to plan, but to be pliant to the least expression of the master's will -- to be a tool in his hand, a chesspiece on the board for him to move just where he willed. And this was the attitude of Elijah's spirit -- surrendered, yielded, emptied; pliant to the hands that reach down out of heaven to mold men.

This attitude is the true one for us all. Are we not too fond of doing things for God, instead of letting God do what He chooses through us? We say, "We will go yonder, we will do this and that, we will work for God thus." We do not consider that we should first inquire if this is God's will for us. We do not recognize His absolute ownership. We often miss doing what He sorely wants us to do, because we insist on carrying out some little whim of our own. This is the blight on much of the activity of Christian people at the present time. They are not satisfied to be as the apostle Paul was, "the servant of Jesus Christ" (Rom_1:1).

Elijah Was Eagerly Desirous to Know and Work Out God's Plan

"Let it be known this day that thou art God in Israel; and that I am thy servant; and that I have done all these things at thy word" (1Ki_18:36). When one feels that he is working out God's plan, and that God is working out His plan through him, he in invincible. Men, circumstances, opposition, are of no more account than the chaff of the autumn threshings. God's plan is His purpose. And God's purpose shall be accomplished; though earth and heaven pass away. And this was doubtless one element in Elijah's splendid strength.

The question of our relation to God's plan is most important, because the power and blessing of God are only to be enjoyed in all their fullness by those who are where He would have them be. God had the plan of the desert wanderings in His thought long before Israel left Egypt, and He worked out that plan by the movements of the cloud over the desert sands. The manna fell on any given morning only where the cloud was brooding, shielding the host by its fleecy fold. To get the manna and the shade, the blood-redeemed must be just where God's plan required them to be. This is a parable of our lives. Would we have divine supplies? We must keep step with the divine plan. The fire burns only when we erect the altar according to God's word. We must not be disobedient to a heavenly vision. We must not spend our years in daydreams, nor in seeking comfort; but must be incessant in uttering the cry, "What wilt Thou have me to do?"

There are many ways of learning God's plan. Sometimes it is revealed in circumstances -- not always pleasant, but ever acceptable, because they reveal our Father's will. No circumstance happens outside His permission; each is a King's messenger bearing His message, though we are sometimes puzzled to decipher it. Sometimes God's plan is revealed by strong impressions of duty, which increase in proportion as they are prayed over and tested by the Word of God.

There are many voices by which God can speak His will to the truly surrendered spirit. If there is any confusion as to what it is, it is due to one of these two causes: either the human will is not fully yielded to do God's will so soon as it is known, but there is some film between the two, preventing the entire permeation of the human by the Divine; or the time of perfect knowledge has not arrived, and we must be content to wait quietly. It is a true rule for us all, to do nothing so long as we are in any uncertainty; but to examine ourselves and be ready to act as soon as we know. We may have the experience of the apostle Peter repeated in our own: "While Peter doubted in himself what this vision which he had seen should mean, behold, the men... sent from Cornelius... stood before the gate" (Act_10:17). The knocking of three men at a gate may sometimes indicate God's plan, or a dream from across the sea, or the glimpse of a weary face, just a little more weary than others around (Act_16:9-10; Joh_5:6-7).

The plan, as Elijah unfolded it to Ahab, was eminently adapted to the circumstances of the case. All Israel was to be gathered by royal summons to Carmel, which reared itself above the plain of Esdraelon, a noble site for a national meeting ground. Special care was to be taken to secure the presence of the representatives of the systems that had dared to rival the worship of Jehovah: "The prophets of Baal four hundred and fifty, and the prophets of the groves four hundred, which eat at Jezebel's table" (1Ki_18:19). A test was then to be imposed on these rival systems, which the adherents of Baal could not possibly refuse, for he was the sun-god, and this was a trial by fire.

Elijah know that the altar of Baal would remain smokeless. He knew that Jehovah would answer his faith by fire, as He had done again and again in the glorious past. He felt convinced also that the people, unable to escape the evidence of their senses, would forever disavow the accursed systems of Phoenicia and return once more to the worship of the God of their fathers.

It is probably that, in the case of Ahab, only so much of this plan was disclosed as was necessary to secure the gathering of the people. To tell him too much would be to invite criticism and perhaps to arouse opposition. It is not likely that he would have been so pliant unless allured by the bait of rain. "So Ahab sent unto all the children of Israel, and gathered the prophets together unto mount Carmel" (1Ki_18:20).

We do not know how this was done, but doubtless the royal word would be passed through the country by a system of messengers, like those which once gave warning of the peril of Jabesh-Gilead or, in later times, carried the fiery cross through the highlands. But in any case this summoning of the people must have taken a few days. And it is by that interval of waiting that we are for a moment arrested. It was like the sultry hush which precedes the breaking of a tropical thunderstorm, or the momentary pause before long lines of armed men are launched at each other in the shock of battle.

Where and how did Elijah spend that interval? We are told that "he came unto all the people," when they were finally assembled on the appointed day. We may not press the word, but does it not suggest that he came from the contrary direction to that from which the people gathered? And if the people came from the whole circumference of the land, may he not have come from some ancient cave of Carmel's heights, just where the long range of hills drops suddenly down in sheer precipices on the sea?

In my opinion, Elijah spent those memorable days of waiting on Carmel itself; sheltering himself and the lad in some wild cave at night, and by day going carefully over the scene of the approaching conflict. How mournfully would he bend over the stones of the altar, which was broken down! It was broken down not by the wild weather, or the devastating hand of time, but by the wicked behest of Jezebel (1Ki_18:32). How eagerly would he search out the original twelve stones, strewn recklessly afar and covered by wild undergrowth. He would need them soon! How constantly would he stay himself upon his God and pour out litanies of supplication for the people and gird himself for the coming conflict by effectual, fervent prayer. Would he not learn the way down to Kishon's brook beneath, and visit the perennial spring from which he would fill the barrels again and yet again with water?

We sometimes seem to think that that answer of fire was probably so much the result of God's determination as to have been largely independent of any special exercise of the prophet's faith. We suppose that more faith and prayer were needed to bring the rain than to bring the leaping, consuming flame. We consider that the one needed the intense sevenfold prayer, while the other needed only the few sentences spoken in the audience of the amazed people, at the moment of sacrifice. But this is a very superficial reading of the story. It is not in harmony with the general dealings of God. As much fervent, believing prayer was needed for the fire as for the rain, and the answer by fire would never have some that day if the previous days had not been spent in the presence-chamber of God. The prayer during ten days of waiting, in the upper room, must precede the descent of the Holy Ghost, as a baptism of fire, on the day of Pentecost.

It is a sublime spectacle -- this yielded, surrendered man, waiting on Carmel in steadfast faith; the gathering of the people; and the unfolding of the purpose of God. He had no fear about the issue, and as the days rolled by, his soul rose in higher and ever higher joy. He expected soon to see a nation at the feet of God.

And he was all this, not because he was of a different make to ourselves; but because he had got into the blessed habit of dealing with God at first hand, as a living reality, in whose presence it was his privilege and glory always to stand.

Chapter Eight - The Conflict on the Heights of Carmel

It is early morning upon Mount Carmel. We are standing on the highest point, looking northward to where Hermon, on the extreme borders of the land, rears its snowcapped head to heaven. Around us on the left lies the Mediterranean Sea, its deep blue waters flocked here and there by the sails of the Tyrian mariners. Immediately at Carmel's base winds Kishon's ancient brook, once choked by the slaughter of Sisera's host. Beyond it stretches the plain of Esdraelon, the garden of Palestine, now sere and barren with three years' drought. Away there in the distance is the city of Jezreel, with the royal palace and the idol temple distinctly visible.

From all sides the crowds are making their way toward this spot, which, from the remotest times, has been associated with worship. No work is being done anywhere. The fires are dying out in the smithy and the forge. The instruments of labor hang useless on the walls. the whole thought of young and old is concentrated on that mighty convocation to which Ahab has summoned them. See how the many thousands of Israel are slowly gathering and taking up every spot of vantage ground from which a view can be obtained of the proceedings; and prepared for any extreme -- from the impure rites of Baal and Astarte, to the reestablishment of their fathers' religion on the dead bodies of the false priests!

The people are nearly gathered, and there is the regular tread of marshaled men -- four hundred prophets of Baal, conspicuous with the sun symbols flashing on their brows. But the prophets of Astarte are absent.

The queen, at whose table they ate, has overruled the summons of the king. And now, through the crowd, the litter of the king, borne by stalwart carriers, threads its way, surrounded by the great officers of state.

But our thought turns from the natural panorama, and the sea of upturned faces, and the flashing splendor of the priests, sure of court favor, and insolently defiant. We fix our thought with intense interest on that one man, of sinewy build and flowing hair, who, with flashing eye and compressed lip, awaits the quiet hush which will presently fall upon that mighty concourse. One man against a nation! See with what malignant glances his every movement is watched by the priests. No tiger ever watched its victim more fiercely! If they had their way, he would never touch yonder plain again.

The king alternates between fear and hate, but restrains himself. He feels that, somehow, the coming of the rain depends on this one man. And through the crowd, if there be sympathizers, they are hushed and still. Even Obadiah discreetly keeps out of the way. But do not fear for Elijah -- he needs no sympathy! He is consciously standing in the presence of One to whom the nations of men are as grasshoppers. All heaven is at his back. Legions of angels fill the mountain with horses and chariots of fire. He is only a man of like passions with ourselves, but he is full of faith and spiritual power. He has learned the secret of moving God Himself. He can avail of the very resources of Deity, as a slender rod may draw lightning from the cloud. This very day -- not by any inherent power, but by faith -- you shall see him subdue a kingdom, work righteousness, escape the edge of the sword, wax valiant in the fight, and turn armies of aliens to flight. Nothing shall be impossible to him. Is it not written that "All things are possible to him that believeth"? (Mar_9:23). He spoke seven times during the course of that memorable day, and his times during the course of that memorable day, and his words are the true index of what was passing in his heart.

Elijah Uttered a Remonstrance

"Elijah came unto all the people, and said, How long halt ye between two opinions? if the LORD be God, follow him; but if Baal, then follow him" (1Ki_18:21). To his clear faith, which was almost sight, there was no IF. He did not doubt for a moment that the LORD was God. But he wanted to show the people the absurdity of their position. Religions so diametrically opposed could not both be right. One of them must be wrong. As soon as the true one was discovered, the one shown to be false must be cast to the winds.

49

At present their position was illogical and absurd. Their course was like the limp of a man whose legs are uneven, or like the device of a servant employed to serve two masters -- doing his best for both and failing to please either. His sincere and simple soul had no patience with such egregious folly. No doubt they had drifted into it, as men often do drift into absurd and wrong positions. We are all liable to that drift of the stream. But the time had come for the nation to be arrested in its attempt to mingle the worship of Jehovah and Baal and compelled to choose between the two issues that presented themselves. Undoubtedly, the prophet felt that once his people were compelled to choose between the two and to say whether the Jehovah of their fathers, or Baal should be God, there should be no doubt as to their verdict.

The people seemed to have been stunned and ashamed that such alternatives should be presented to their choice, for "the people answered him not a word" (1Ki_18:21). Oh, for the clear- sightedness of that faith which shall show men the unreasonableness of their position -- sweeping away the cobwebs of sophistry with a single movement of the hand and arraigning them at the bar of their own consciences, silent and condemned. It is needed in our day as much as ever. Everywhere men are trying to win the smile of the world and the "well done" of Christ. They crowd alike the temples of mammon and of God. They try to be popular in the court of Saul, and to stand well with the exiled David.

Elijah Threw Down a Challenge

"The God that answereth by fire, let him be God." It was a fair proposal, because Baal was the lord of the sun and the god of those productive natural forces of which heat is the element and sign. The votaries of Baal could not therefore refuse.

And every Israelite could recall many an occasion in the glorious past when Jehovah had answered by fire. It burned in the acacia bush which was its own fuel. It shone like a beacon light in the van of the desert march. It gleamed on the brow of Sinai. It smote the murmuring crowds. It fell upon the sacrifices which awaited it on the brazen altar. It was the emblem of Jehovah, and the sign of His acceptance of His people's service.

When Elijah proposed that each side should offer a bullock and await an answer by fire, he secured the immediate acquiescence of the people. "All the people answered and said, It is well spoken" (1Ki_18:24).

That proposal was made in the perfect assurance that God would not fail him. Had he not spend days in prayer? Had not the divine plan been

50

revealed to him? Was it to be supposed for a moment that God would push His servant into the front of the battle, and then leave him? Granted that a miracle must be wrought before the sun set: there was no difficulty about that to a man who lived in the secret place of the Most High. Miracles are only the results of the higher laws of His chamber.

God will never fail the man who trusts Him utterly. He may keep him waiting until the fourth watch of the morning, but the gray dawn will reveal Him stepping across the billows' crests to His servant's help. Be sure that you are on God's plan, then forward in God's name! The very elements shall obey you, and fire shall leap from heaven at your command.

Elijah Dealt Out Withering Sarcasm

For the first time in their existence, the false priests were unable to insert the secret spark of fire among the fagots that lay upon their altar. They were compelled, therefore, to rely on a direct appeal to their patron deity. And this they did with might and main. Round and round the altar they went in the mystic choric dance, breaking their rank sometimes by an excited leap up and down at the altar which was made; and all the while repeating the monotonous chant, "O Baal, hear us!" (1Ki_18:26). But there was no voice, nor any that answered. "Their idols are silver and gold, the work of men's hands. They have mouths, but they speak not: eyes have they, but they see not: they have ears, but they hear not:... they that make them are like unto them, so is everyone that trusteth in them" (Psa_115:4-6; Psa_115:8).

Three hours passed. Their deity slowly drove his golden chariot up the steep of heaven and ascended his throne in the zenith. It was surely the time of his greatest power, and he must help them then if ever. But all he did was to bronze the eager, upturned faces of his priests to a deeper tint.

Elijah could ill conceal his delight in their defeat. He knew it would be so. He was so sure that nothing could avert their utter discomfiture that he could afford to mock them by suggesting a cause for the indifference of their god: "Cry aloud: for he is a god; either he is talking, or he is pursuing, or he is in a journey, or peradventure he sleepeth, and must be awaked" (1Ki_18:27). Sarcasm is an invaluable weapon when it is used to expose the ridiculous pretensions of error and convince men of the folly and unreasonableness of their ways.

"And they cried aloud, and cut themselves after their manner with knives and lancets, till the blood gushed out upon them" (1Ki_18:28).

51

Surely their extremity was enough to touch the compassion of any deity, however hard to move! And, since the heavens still continued dumb, did it not prove to the people that their religion was a delusion and a sham?

Three more hours passed by, until the hour had come when, in the temple of Jerusalem, the priests of God were accustomed to offer the evening lamb. But "There was neither voice, nor any to answer, nor any that regarded (1Ki_18:29). The altar stood cold and smokeless, the bullock unconsumed.

Elijah Issued an Invitation

His time had come at last, and his first act was to invite the people nearer. He knew what his faith and prayer had won from God, but he wanted the answer of fire to be beyond dispute. He therefore invited the close scrutiny of the people as he reared the broken altar of the Lord. As he sought, with reverent care, those scattered stones and built them together so that the twelve stood as one -- a meet symbol of the unity of the ideal Israel in the sight of God -- the keen glances of the people in his close proximity could see that there was no inserted torch or secret spark.

Do we not want a few more, who, amid the scatterings of the present day, can still discern the true unity of the Church, the Body of Christ? We may never see that unity visibly manifested until we see the Bride, the Lamb's wife, descend out of heaven from God, having the glory of God. But nevertheless we can enter into God's ideal of it as a spiritual unity, existing unbroken in His thought and unaffected by the divisions of our times. Is it not clear that, during this age, the Church of Christ was never meant to be a visible corporate body, but a great spiritual reality, consisting of all faithful and loyal spirits, in all communions, who, holding the Head, are necessarily one with each other?

Elijah Gave a Command

His faith was exuberant. He was so sure of God, that he dared to heap difficulties in His way, knowing that there is no real difficulty for infinite power. The more unlikely the answer was, the more glory would there be to God. Oh, matchless faith! which can laugh at impossibilities and heap them one upon another, to have the pleasure of seeing God vanquish them -- as a steam hammer cracks a nutshell placed under it by the wondering child.

The altar was reared, the wood laid in order, the bullock cut in pieces; but to prevent any possibility of fraud and make the coming miracle still more wonderful, Elijah said, "Fill four barrels with water, and pour it on the sacrifice and on the wood (1Ki_18:33). This they did three times until the wood was drenched, and the water filled the trench, making it impossible for a spark to travel across.

Alas, few of us have faith like this! We are not so sure of God that we dare to pile difficulties in His way. We all try our best to make it easy for Him to help us. Yet what this man had, we too may have, by prayer and fasting.

Elijah Offered a Prayer

Such a prayer! It was quiet and assured, confident of an answer. Its chief burden was that God should vindicate Himself that day, showing Himself to be God indeed and turning the people's heart back to Himself.

Whenever we can so lose ourselves in prayer as to forget personal interests and to plead for the glory of God, we have reached a vantage ground from which we can win anything from Him. Our blessed Lord, in His earthly life, had but one passion -- that His Father might be glorified; and now He cannot resist fulfilling the prayer which advances this as its plea: "Whatsoever ye shall ask in my name, that will I do, that the Father may be glorified in the Son" (Joh_14:13).

Is it wonderful that "the fire of the Lord fell and consumed the burnt-sacrifice, and the wood, and the stones, and the dust, and licked up the water that was in the trench" (1Ki_18:38)? It could not have been otherwise! And let us not think that this is an old-world tale, never to be repeated. The fire still waits for the Promethean faith that can bring it down. If there were the same need, and if any one of us exercised the same faith, we might again see fire descending. Did not the Holy Ghost inaugurate this very age with flames of fire? Our God is a consuming fire and when the unity of His people is once recognized, and His presence is sought, He will descend, overcoming all obstacles and converting a drenched and dripping sacrifice into food on which He Himself can feed.

Elijah Issued an Order for Execution

It was a very terrible act, and yet what could he do? The saints of those times knew nothing of our false notions of liberality. Tell Elijah that those men might be sincere; he would find it difficult to believe it. He would assert that they were none the less dangerous to the best interests of his people. To let them escape would be to license them as the agents of apostasy. They must die. And so the order went forth from those stern lips: "Take the prophets of Baal; let not one of them escape" (1Ki_18:40). The people were in the mood to obey. Only a moment before they had rent the air with the shout, "The LORD, he is the God; the LORD, he is the God (1Ki_18:39). They had seen how hideously they had been deceived. And now they close round the cowed and vanquished priests, who see that resistance is in vain, and their hour has come.

"And they took them" (1Ki_18:40). Some took one, and some another. Each priest was hurried down he mountainside by the frenzied and determined men who were beginning to see them as the cause of the long drought.

"Elijah brought them down to the brook Kishon, and slew them there" (1Ki_18:40). One after another they fell beneath his sword while the king stood by, a helpless spectator of their doom, and Baal did naught to save them.

And when the last was dead, the prophet knew that rain was not far off. He could almost hear the clouds hurrying toward the land. He knew what we all need to know; that God can only bless the land or heart which no longer shelters within its borders rivals to Himself. May God clear us of His rivals and impart to us Elijah's faith, that we may also be strong and do exploits!

Chapter Nine - Rain at Last!

We can, to a very inadequate degree, realize the horrors of an Eastern drought. And it would have been difficult in the parched land on which Elijah gazed from Carmel, to have recognized that garden of the Lord of which Moses said: "The LORD thy God bringeth thee into a good land, a land of brooks of water, of fountains and depths that spring out of valleys and hills; a land wherein thou shalt eat bread without scarceness, thou shalt not lack any thing in it" (Deu_8:7; Deu_8:9).

But beside this exquisite delineation, Moses had been given a description of the certain calamities that would ensue if Israel went aside from any of the words which God commanded, to the right hand or to the left. And among other items of misery, it was expressly stated that the heaven overhead should be brass, and the earth underfoot iron, and the very rain should be transformed to powder and dust (Deu_28:23-24). This terrible prediction had now been literally fulfilled. And the anguish of the land was directly attributable to the apostasy of its people. All this was the result of sin. The iniquities of Israel had separated between them and their God. Elijah knew this, and it prompted him to act the part of executioner to the priests of Baal. They had been the ringleaders in the national revolt from God, but their bodies now lay in ghastly death on the banks of the Kishon, or were being hurried out to sea.

Ahab must have stood by Elijah in the Kishon gorge, an unwilling spectator of that fearful deed of vengeance, not daring to resist the outburst of popular indignation or attempt to shield the men whom he had himself encouraged and introduced. When the last priest had bitten the dust, Elijah turned to the king and said, "Get thee up, eat and drink; for there is a sound of abundance of rain" (1Ki_18:41). It was as if he said, "Get thee up to where thy tents are pitched on yon broad upland sweep; the feast is spread in thy gilded pavilion; thy lackeys await thee; feast thee on thy dainties; but be quick! for now that the land is rid of these traitor priests, and God is once more enthroned in His rightful place, the showers of rain cannot be longer delayed. Can you not hear the sough of the western breeze, which shall soon become a hurricane? Be quick! or the rain may interrupt thy carouse."

What a contrast between these two men! "Ahab went up to eat and drink. And Elijah went up to the top of Carmel; and he cast himself down upon the earth, and put his face between his knees" (1Ki_18:42). It is no more than we might have expected of the king. When his people were suffering the extremities of drought, he cared only to find grass enough to save his stud. Now, though his faithful priests had died by hundreds, he thought only of the banquet that awaited him in his pavilion. Cruel, cowardly, mean, and sensual are the least epithets we can apply to this worthless man, clad though he was with he royal robes of Israel. I think I can see Ahab and Elijah ascending those heights together: no sympathy, no common joy, no reciprocated thanksgiving. The king turns straight off to his tents while the servant of God climbs to the highest part of the mountain and finds an oratory at the base of a yet higher spur from which a marvelous view could be obtained of the broad expanse of the Mediterranean, which slept under the growing stillness of the coming night.

Such contrasts still reveal themselves. Crises reveal the secrets of men's hearts and show of what stuff they are made. The children of this world will spend their days in feasting, and their nights in revelry, though a world is rushing down to ruin. If only they can eat and drink, they are regardless of the needs of the perishing and the judgments of God. Such feasted with Belshazzar when the foe was at the gates of Babylon. Such filled with the frivolities the royal apartments of Whitehall when William of Orange was landing at Tor Bay. And woe to the land when such men rule! The sequence between the sensual luxury of the rulers and the decadence of the nation was well pointed out by Isaiah when he said: "Woe unto them that rise up early in the morning, that they may follow strong drink; that tarry late into the night, till wine inflame them! And the harp and the lute, the tabret and the pipe, and wine, are in their feasts: but they regard not the work of the LORD, neither have they considered the operation of his hands. Therefore my people are gone into captivity" (Isa_5:11-13 RV). May our beloved country be preserved from having such leaders as these! And may our youth be found, not garlanded and scented for the Ahab feasts, but with Elijah on the bleak uplands; where there may be no dainty viands, but where the air is fresh, and life is free, and the spirit is braced to noble deeds.

There are certain characteristics in Elijah's prayer, which we must notice as we pass, because they should form part of all true prayer.

IT WAS BASED ON THE PROMISE OF GOD.

When Elijah was summoned from Zarephath to resume his public work, his marching orders were capped by the specific promise of rain: "Go, show thyself unto Ahab; and I will send rain upon the earth" (1Ki_18:1). To natural reason this might have seemed to render prayer unnecessary. Would not God fulfill His promise, and send the rain, altogether irrespective of further prayer? But Elijah's spiritual instincts argued otherwise, and more truly. Though he had never heard the words, yet he anticipated the thought of a later prophet who, after enunciating all that God was prepared to do for His people, uttered these significant words: "Thus saith the Lord God, I will yet for this be inquired of by the house of Israel, to do it for them."

God's promises are given, not to restrain, but to incite to prayer. They show the direction in which we may ask, and the extent to which we may expect an answer. They are the mold into which we may pour our fervid spirits without fear. They are the signed check, made payable to order, which we must endorse and present for payment. Though the Bible is crowded with golden promises from board to board, yet will they be inoperative until we turn them into prayer. It is not our province to argue the reasonableness of this; it is enough to argue and enforce it. Why should it not be sufficient to silence all questions by saying that we have here reached one of the primal laws of the spiritual world, as simple, as certain, as universal, as any that obtain in the world of nature? Promises of abundant harvest smile to the husbandman from earth and sky, but he knows that they will not be realized unless he puts into operation the laws and processes of agriculture. As he does so, it is not necessary for his success that he should understand the why and wherefore; it is enough for him to do his little part, and he finds that every promise is fulfilled in the produce shed at his feet from Nature's golden horn.

When, therefore, we are asked why men should pray, and how prayer avails, we are not careful to answer more than this: "Prayer is the instinct of the religious life; it is one of the first principles of the spiritual world." It is clearly taught in the Word of God to be prevalent with the Almighty. It has been practiced by the noblest and saintliest of men, who have testified to its certain efficacy. Our Lord Jesus not only practiced it, but proclaimed its value in words which have been plunged a myriad times into the crucible of experience and are as true today as ever: "Ask, and it shall be given you; seek, and ye shall find; knock, and it shall be opened unto you" (Luk_11:9). We are content, therefore, to pray, though we are as ignorant of the philosophy of the modus operandi of prayer as we are of any natural law. We find it no dreamy reverie or sweet sentimentality, but a practical, living force. Whenever we stand by the altar of incense, we become aware of the angel of the Lord standing hard by, and saying, "Fear not, O man greatly beloved! thy prayer is heard."

When your child was a toddling, lisping babe, he asked many things wholly incompatible with your nature and its own welfare; but as the years have passed, increasing experience has molded your child's requests into shapes suggested by yourself. So, as we know more of God through His promises, we are staid from asking what He cannot give and led to set our hearts on things which lie on His open palm waiting to be taken by the hand of an appropriating faith. This is why all prayer, like Elijah's, should be based on promise. We stand on a foundation of adamant and have an irresistible purchase with God when we can put our finger on His own promise and say, "Do as Thou hast said."

IT WAS DEFINITE.

This is where so many prayers fail. They are shot like arrows into the air. They are like letters which require no answer because they ask for nothing. They are like the firing of artillery in a mimic fight when only gunpowder is employed. This is why they are so wanting in power and interest. We do not pray with an expectation of attaining definite and practical results. We wander out like Isaac to meditate in the fields at eventide, but we fail to ascend Carmel with the compressed lip and the resolute step of Elijah, as determined, if we may, to win by prayer the fulfillment of some blessed promise, as he was to bring the longed-for rain. Let us amend in this matter. Let us keep a list of petitions which we shall plead before God. Let us direct our prayer, as David did (Psa_5:3), and look up for the answer; and we shall find ourselves obtaining new and unwonted blessings. Be definite!

IT WAS EARNEST.

"Elias... prayed earnestly" (Jas_5:17). This is the testimony of the Holy Spirit, through the apostle James. It was the effectual, fervent prayer of a righteous man, which availeth much. The prayers of Scripture all glow with the white heat of intensity. Remember how Jacob wrestled, and David panted and poured out his soul; the importunity of the blind beggar, and the persistency of the distracted mother; the strong crying and tears of our Lord. In each case the whole being seemed gathered up, as a stone into a catapult, and hurled forth in vehement entreaty. Prayer is only answered for the glory of Christ, but it is not answered unless it be accompanied with such earnestness as will

prove that the blessing sought is really needed.

Ah, what earnestness pants and throbs on every side! No listless attention! No flagging interest! No drowsy eye! Oh, for such violence, guided by holiness, to take the kingdom of heaven by force! Such earnestness is, of course, to be dreaded when we seek some lower boon for ourselves. But when, like Elijah, we seek the fulfillment of the divine promise -- not for ourselves, but for the glory of God -- then it is impossible to be too much in earnest or too full of the energy of prayer.

ELIJAH'S PRAYER WAS HUMBLE.

"He cast himself down on the ground, and put his face between his knees." We scarcely recognize him, he seems to have so lost his identity. A few hours before, he stood erect as an oak of Bashan; now, he is bowed as a bulrush. Then as God's ambassador he pleaded with man; now as man's intercessor he pleads with God. Is it not always so -- that the men who stand straightest in the presence of sin bow lowest in the presence of God? And is it not also true, that those who live nearest God are the most reverent? True, you are a child; but you are also a subject. True, you are a redeemed man; but you can never forget your original name, sinner. True, you may come with boldness; but remember the majesty, might, and power of God, and take your shoes off. The angels of His presence fly with veiled faces to do His bidding, as they cry, "Holy, Holy, Holy!" The most tender love, which casts out the tormenting fear, begets a fear that is as sensitive as that of John who, though he lay his head on Jesus' breast, scrupled too hastily to intrude upon the grave where He had slept. Our only plea with God is the merit and blood of our great High Priest. It becomes us to be humble.

IT WAS FULL OF EXPECTANT FAITH.

"What things soever ye desire, when ye pray, believe that ye receive them, and ye shall have them" (Mar_11:24). Faith is the indispensable condition of all true prayer. It is the gift of the Holy Ghost. It thrives by exercise. It grows strong by feeding on the promises: the Word of God is its natural food. It beat strongly in Elijah's heart. He knew that God would keep His word, and so he sent the lad -- possibly the widows' son -- up to the highest point of Carmel and bade him look toward the sea. He was sure that before long his prayer would be answered, and God's promise would be kept. We have often prayed and failed to look out for the blessings we have sought. The stately ships of heaven have come up to the quays, laden with the very blessings we asked; but as we have not been there to welcome and unload them, they have put out again to sea. The messenger pigeons have come back again to their cotes with the tiny messages concealed beneath their wings, but we have not been there to search for them and take them.

Sometimes we have to exercise faith on the simple warrant of God's Word. At other times, God seems to give us special faith for things which are not directly promised. THe presence or absence of faith is a great test in prayer. Where it is present, we are so sure of the answer as to turn petition into thanksgiving. But where it is persistently absent, and where continued prayer fails to light up the spirit with the conviction of coming answer, then it would seem as if the Urim and Thummim stone is darkening with one of God's loving refusals and He says, "Ask me no more concerning this matter."

There is a faith which God cannot refuse; to which all things are possible; which laughs at impossibility; which can move mountains and plant them in the sea. May such faith be ours! It can be ours only by careful and eager nurture. Such faith was Elijah's.

IT WAS VERY PERSEVERING.

He said to his servant, "Go up now, look toward the sea." And he went up, and looked, and said, "There is nothing." --How often have we sent the lad of eager desire to scan the horizon! and how often has he returned with the answer, There is nothing!-- There is no tear of penitence in those hard eyes. There is no symptom of amendment in that wild life. There is no sign of deliverance in these sore perplexities. There is nothing. And because there is nothing when we have just begun to pray, we leave off praying. We leave the mountain brow. We do not know that God's answer is even then upon the way.

Not so with Elijah. "And he said, Go again seven times" (1Ki_18:43). There is a truer rendering of this: "Then said he seven times, Go again." It is not that the lad was told to run to and fro seven times, without interrupting the prophet in prayer; but it would appear that again and again the lad came back to his master with the same message. "There is nothing;" and, after an interval, he was bidden to go again.

He came back the first time, saying, "There is nothing" (1Ki_18:43). Elijah said, "Go again." And that was repeated seven times. It was no small test of the prophet's endurance; but he was not tried more than he could endure, and with the ordeal there came sufficient grace, so that he was able to bear it.

Not unfrequently our Father grants our prayer, and labels the answer for us; but He keeps it back, that we may be led on to a point of intensity, which shall bless our spirits forever, and from which we shall never recede. The psalmist says, "Yea, let none that wait on thee be ashamed" (Psa_25:3). Then when we have outdone ourselves, He lovingly turns to us, and says, "Great is thy faith: be it unto thee even as thou wilt!" (Mat_15:28). He waits, that He may be gracious unto us.

AND THE PRAYER WAS ABUNDANTLY ANSWERED.

For weeks and months before, the sun had been gathering drops of mist from lake and river, from sea and ocean, drawing them as clouds in coronets of glory and around himself. Now the gale was bearing them rapidly toward the thirsty land of Israel. "Before they call, I will answer; and while they are yet speaking, I will hear" (Isa_65:24). The answer to your prayers may be nearer than you think. It may already have started by the down-line. On the wings of every moment it is hastening toward you. God shall answer you, and that right early.

Presently the lad, from his tower of observation, beheld on the horizon a tiny cloud, no bigger than a man's hand, scudding across the sky. No more was needed to convince an Oriental that rain was near. It was, and is, the certain precursor of a sudden hurricane of wind and rain. The lad was sent with an urgent message to Ahab, to descend from Carmel to his chariot in the plain beneath, lest Kishon, swollen by the rains, should stop him in his homeward career. The lad had barely time to reach the royal pavilion before the heavens were black with clouds and wind, and there was a great rain.

The monarch started amid the pelting storm, but fleeter than his swift steeds were the feet of the prophet, energized by the hand of God. He snatched up his streaming mantel and twisted it around his loins. Amid the fury of the elements with which the night closed in, he outstripped the chariot and ran like a common courier before it to the entrance of Jezreel, some eighteen miles distant. He did this to convince the king that in his zeal against idolatry he was actuated by no personal disrespect to himself and prompted only by jealousy for God.

Thus by his faith and prayer this solitary man brought back the rain to Israel. More things are wrought by prayer than this world knows of. Why should not we learn and practice his secret? It is certainly within the reach of us all. Then we too might bring spiritual blessings from heaven, which should make the parched places of the church and the world rejoice and blossom as the rose.

Chapter Ten - How the Mighty Fell!

Amid the drenching storm with which the memorable day of the convocation closed in, the king and the prophet reached Jezreel. Probably they were the first to bring tidings of what had occurred. Elijah went to some humble lodging for shelter and food, while Ahab repaired to the palace, where Jezebel awaited him. All day long the queen had been wondering how matters were going on Mount Carmel. She cherished the feverish hope that her priests had won the day; and when she saw the rain-clouds steal over the sky, she attributed the welcome change so some great interposition of Baal in answer to their pleadings. May not some such colloquy as this have taken place between the royal pair, when they met in the palace interior?

"How have things gone today? No doubt, well; the rain has anticipated your favorable reply."

"I have nothing to tell you that will give you pleasure."

"Why! Has anything happened?"

"The worst has happened."

"What do you mean? Where are my priests?"

"You will never see them again."

"Never see them again! What do you mean? Tell me quickly!"

"They are all dead. By this time their bodies are floating out to sea."

"Who has dared to do this thing? Did they not defend themselves? Did you not raise your hand? How did they die? Where is Elijah? Have the people broken into revolt?"

Then "Ahab told Jezebel all that Elijah had done and withal how he had slain all the prophets with the sword" (1Ki_19:1).

Jezebel's indignation knew no bounds. She was like a tigress robbed of her young. Ahab's temperament was sensual and materialistic. If he had enough to eat and drink, and the horses and mules were cared for, he wan content. He could not understand people becoming so enthusiastic about religious matters. In his judgment there was not much to choose between God and Baal. His was the motto of the Epicurean, "Let us eat and drink; for tomorrow we die." Not so Jezebel. She was as resolute as he was indifferent. Crafty, unscrupulous, and intriguing, she molded Ahab to her mind; and, in doing so, anticipated the symbol of the Apocalypse in which the scarlet-clad woman rides upon the beast.

To Jezebel the crisis was one of gravest moment. Policy, as well as indignation, prompted her to act at once. If this national reformation were permitted to spread, it would sweep away before it all that she had been laboring at for years. She must strike, and strike at once; and where would her blow tell so well as when aimed at the master-spirit of the day's proceedings? So that very night, amid the violence of the storm, she sent a messenger to Elijah, saying, "So let the gods do to me, and more also, if I make not thy life as the life of one of them, by tomorrow about this time" (1Ki_19:2). That message betrays the woman. She did not dare to kill him, though he was easily within her power. So she mastered her wrath, and contented herself with threats. Her mind was set on driving him from the country, so she might be left free to repair the havoc he had caused. In this, alas! she was only too successful.

Elijah's presence had never been so necessary as now. The work of destruction had commenced, and the people were in a mood to carry it through to the bitter end. The tide had turned and was setting in toward God. Elijah was needed to direct its flow, to keep the people true to the choice which they had made, and to complete the work of reformation by a work of construction. From what we have seen of him, we should have expected that he would receive the message with unruffled composure, laying it before God in quiet confidence, assured that He would hide him in the secret of His Pavilion from the wrath of man and shield him from the strife of tongues. Surely he will preserve a dignified silence or return an answer like that which Chrysostom sent on a similar occasion to the Empress Eudoxia, "Go tell her I fear nothing but sin." But, instead of this, we are told (and surely the sacred historian must have heaved a deep sigh as he wrote the words), "When he saw that, he arose, and went for his life" (1Ki_19:1-21; 1Ki_3:1-28).

He went for his life! Accompanied by his servant, and under covert of the night, he hurried through the driving storm, across the hills of Samaria, and directed his course, with true Bedouin instinct, toward the extreme south of Judea, where the pasture lands of Palestine fade into the drear expanse of the Arabian desert. Nor did he slacken his speed until he had left far behind him the country over which Jezebel's scepter swayed and had reached Beersheba, the town that clustered round the well of the oath -- where, centuries before, Abraham had planted a grove and called upon the name of the Lord. He was safe there, but even there he could not stay. His spirit seems to have become utterly demoralized and panic-stricken. He would not even brook the company of his servant. So, leaving him in Beersheba, he plunged alone into that wild desert waste that stretches southward to Sinai.

Through the weary hours he plodded on beneath the burning sun, his feet blistered by the scorching sands. No ravens, no Cherith, no Zarephath were there. No human sympathy lent him its kindly aid. The very presence of God seemed to have withdrawn itself form his side. At last the fatigue and anguish overpowered even his sinewy strength, and he cast himself beneath the slight shadow of a small shrub of juniper, and asked to die. "It is enough now, O LORD, take away my life; for I am not better than my fathers" (1Ki_19:4).

What might have been! If only Elijah had held his ground -- dwelling in the secret place of the Most High and hiding under the shadow of the Almighty -- he might have saved his country. There would have been no necessity for the captivity and dispersion of his people. The seven thousand secret disciples might have come forth from their hiding places to avow themselves and would have constituted a nucleus of loyal hearts. And his own character would have escaped a stain which has resisted the obliterating erasure of the ages and still remains, fraught with shame and sorrow. Elijah's influence in Israel never recovered from that one false step. He missed a chance which never came again. And though God, in His mercy, treated him lovingly and royally as a child, He never again reinstated him as a servant in just the position which he so thoughtlessly flung away. It is a solemn thought for us all! If for one moment we are left to ourselves, we may take a step which may shatter our influence, and forever after put us into a very different position from that which might have been ours if only we had remained true. As children, we may be forgiven; as servants we are never reinstated or trusted quite as we were once.

It is noteworthy that the Bible saints often fail just where we would have expected them to stand. Abraham was the father of those who believe; but his faith failed him when he went down to Egypt and lied to Pharaoh about his wife. Moses was the meekest of men; but he missed Canaan because he spoke unadvisedly with his lips. John was the apostle of love, yet in a moment of intolerance he wished to call down fire out of heaven. So Elijah, who might have been supposed to be superior to all human weakness, shows himself to be indeed "a man subject to like passions as are we" (Jas_5:17).

The old castle, which from its hill, watches over the town of Edinburgh clustering beneath, was captured only once in the whole history of Scotland, and its capture happened thus: its defenders thought that on one side the steepness of the rock made it inaccessible and impregnable; and they put no sentries there. And so, in the gray mist of the early morning, a little party crept up the precipitous slopes and surprised the garrison into surrender.

Is there not a warning here for us all? It may be that some have been saying boastfully of certain forms of vice, "I shall never yield to this or that. I have no inclination to such forms of sin. This is one of the points in which I am strong to resist." Beware! It may be that the great enemy of souls has a special design in producing in you a sense of false security, that he may assail and vanquish you in the very point in which you deem yourself impregnable, and so forbear to watch.

What a proof is here of the veracity of the Bible! Had it been merely a human composition, its authors would have shrunk from delineating the failure of one of its chief heroes. No artist would think of snapping a column just as it was tapering to its coronal. Men sometimes complain against the Bible for its uncompromising portraitures. Yet, is not this its glory? It holds the mirror up to human nature, that we may learn what is in man that we may none of us despair, and that we may infer that, if God were able to fashion his choicest ware out of such common earth, it is possible for Him to do as much again in the most ignorant and degraded of His children. Is there not even a gleam of comfort to be had out of the woeful spectacle of Elijah's fall? If it had not been for this, we should always have thought of him as being too far removed from us to be in any sense a model. We should have looked on him as we do at the memorials of a race of giants, with whom we have nothing in common. But now, as we see him stretched under the shade of the juniper tree asking for death, behaving himself with more pusillanimity than many among us would have manifested, we feel that he was what he was only by the grace of God, received through faith. And by a similar faith we may appropriate a similar grace to ennoble our mean lives.

Several causes account for his terrible failure.

I - HIS PHYSICAL STRENGTH AND NERVOUS ENERGY WERE COMPLETELY OVERTAXED.

Consider the tremendous strain which he had undergone since leaving the shelter of the quiet home at Zarephath. The long excitement of the convocation, the slaughter of the priests, the intensity of his prayer, the eighteen miles' swift run in front of Ahab's chariot, succeeded by the rapid flight which had hardly been relaxed for a single moment until he cast himself upon the desert sand. All this had resulted in sheer exhaustion. He was suffering keenly from reaction, now that the extreme tension was relaxed, and this counted largely in the unutterable depression under which he was suffering.

We are "fearfully and wonderfully made" (Psa_139:14) and our inner life is very sensitive to our outward conditions. It has been truly said that the most trivial causes -- a heated room, a sunless day, want of exercise or a northern aspect -- will make all the difference between faith and doubt, between courage and indecision. Many who send for the religious teacher would be wiser if they sent for their physician. And if any are conscious of having lost the sunny gladness and buoyant faith of former days, before they speak of the mysterious hidings of God's face or lament their own backslidings, it might be well to inquire if there may not be some physical or nervous cause. And if there be, it will attract not the blame, but the compassionate sympathy of Him who knoweth our frame, and remembereth that we are but dust. When we consider the speed and strain of our times, it is marvelous that there are not more among us suffering from the intolerable depression beneath which Elijah sank on the desert sand.

II - HE WAS KEENLY SENSITIVE TO HIS LONELY POSITION.

"I, even I only, am left" (1Ki_19:10). Some men are born to loneliness. It is the penalty of true greatness. At such a time the human spirit is apt to falter, unless it is sustained by an heroic purpose and by an unfaltering faith. The shadow of that loneliness fell dark on the spirit of our divine Master Himself when he said: "Behold, the hour cometh, yea, is now come, that ye shall be scattered, every man to his own, and shall leave me alone: and yet I am not alone, because the Father is with me" (Joh_16:32). If our Lord shrank in the penumbra of that great eclipse, it is not wonderful that Elijah cowered in its darksome gloom. He might have had the company of his lad, but there is company which is not companionship. We may be more lonely in a crowd than in a desert. We need something more than human beings, we need human hearts and sympathy and love.

III - HE LOOKED AWAY FROM GOD TO CIRCUMSTANCES.

Up to that moment Elijah had been animated by a most splendid faith, because he had never lost sight of God. "He endured as seeing Him who is invisible." Faith always thrives when God occupies the whole field of vision. But when Jezebel's threats reached him, we are told most significantly, "when he saw that, he arose, and went for his life" (1Ki_19:3). In after years, Peter walked on the water until he looked from his Master to the seething waves. "When he saw the wind boisterous, he was afraid; and beginning to sink, he cried, saying, Lord save me!" (Mat_14:3). So here, while Elijah set the Lord always before his face, he did not fear, though an host encamped against him. But when he looked at his peril, he thought more of his life than of God's cause; and was afraid of man that should die, and of the son of man that should be made as grass; and forgot the Lord, his Maker, which made heaven and earth. "When he saw that, he arose, and went for his life."

Let us refuse to look at circumstances, though they roll before us as a Red Sea and howl around us like a storm. Circumstances, natural impossibilities, difficulties, are nothing in the estimation of the soul that is occupied with God. They are as the small dust that settles on a scale and is not considered in the measurement of weight. O men of God, get you up into the high mountain, from which you may obtain a good view of the glorious Land of Promise, and refuse to have your gaze diverted by men or things below!

It is a great mistake to dictate to God. Elijah know not what he said when he told God that he had had enough of life, and asked to die. If God had taken him at his word, he would have died under a cloud; he would never have heard the still small voice; he would never have founded the schools of the prophets, or commissioned Elisha for his work; he would never have swept up to heaven in an equipage of flame.

What a mercy it is that God does not answer all our prayers! How gracious He is in reading their inner meaning, and answering that! This, as we shall see, is what He did for His tired and querulous servant.

How many have uttered those words, "It is enough!" -- the sufferer, weary of long and wearing pain; the wife tied to an inhuman husband, the Christian worker whose efforts seem in vain; "It is enough. Let me come home. The burden is more than I can bear. The lessons are tiresome. School is tedious, and the holidays would be so welcome. I cannot see that anything will be gained by longer delay. It is enough!"

O silly, silly children! Little do we know how much we should miss if God were to do as we request. To die now would be to forego immeasurable blessings which await us within forty days' journey from this; and to die like a dog, instead of sweeping, honored and beloved, through the open gates of heaven. It is better to leave it all in the wise and tender thought of God. He wants us home, but will not let us come till we have learned the last lesson and done the last stroke of work. And we shall yet live to thank Him that He refused to gratify our wish when, in a moment of despondency, we cast ourselves upon the ground, and said, "Let us die. It is enough!"

Chapter Eleven - Loving-kindness Better than Life

The holy apostle, whose earliest lessons of the love of God were conned as he leaned on the bosom of Christ, tells us, in words deep and simple as some translucent lake, that "we have known and believed the love that God hath to us." They are wonderful words for mortals to utter. A lifetime would be well spent if, at its close, we could utter them without exaggeration. But alas, many of us have learned some of our deepest lessons of the love of God in having experienced its gentle kindness amid shortcoming and failure, like that which marred Elijah's course.

That failure, as we have seen, was most disastrous. It inflicted lasting disgrace upon Elijah's reputation. It arrested one of the most hopeful movements that ever visited the land of Israel. It struck panic and discouragement into thousands of hearts which were beginning to gather courage from his splendid zeal. It snapped the only brake by which the headlong descent of Israel to destruction could have been prevented. It brought discredit and rebuke on the cause and name of God. A choir of angels might well have gathered around the truant prophet as he lay upon the desert sand and recited some such mournful words as those with which David lamented the death of Saul and Jonathan on Gilboa's fatal field: "How are the mighty fallen in the midst of the battle! O Jonathan, thou wast slain in thine high places. I am distressed for thee... How are the mighty fallen, and the weapons of war perished!" (2Sa_1:25-27).

If ever it were befitting for a man to reap what he had sown and suffer the consequences of his own misdeeds, it would have been so in the case of Elijah. But God's thoughts are not as man's. He know all the storms of disappointment and broken hope which were sweeping across that noble spirit, as gusts of wind across an inland sea. His eye followed with tender pity every step of His servant's flight across the hills of Samaria. He did not love him less than when he stood, elated with victory, by the burning sacrifice. And His love assumed, if possible, a tenderer, gentler aspect as He stooped over Elijah while he slept. As a shepherd tracks the wondering sheep from the fold to the wild mountain pass where eagles, sailing in narrowing circles, watch its faltering steps, so did the love of God come upon Elijah as, worn in body by long fatigue and in spirit by the fierce war of passion, he lay and slept under the juniper tree.

And God did more than love him. He sought, by tender helpfulness, to heal and restore His servant's soul to its former health and joy. At His command, an angel, twice over, prepared a meal upon the desert sand

and touched him and bade him eat. No upbraiding speeches, no word of reproach, no threats of dismissal, but only sleep and food and kindly thoughtfulness of the great journey which he was bent on making to Horeb, the mount of God. It makes us think of Him who, in after days, prepared in the early morning upon the shore of the lake, a breakfast such as wet and weary fishermen would love -- there was a fire, and fish laid thereon, and bread. And He did this for those who, following the impulsive lead of Peter, had apparently determined to wait no more for His coming but to return to the boats and fishing-tackle from which He had called them three years before.

It may be that these words will be read by those who have failed. You once avowed yourselves to be the Lord's; and lived for a little on the uplands where the golden light ever shines upon the happy spirit. Or perhaps you professed to enter the blessed life, and you did taste its joys and experience its liberty and victory. Or maybe you have stood up to teach others, stirring them to deeds of heroic courage and daring. But all that is over now. You have fallen, as Milton's Archangel, from heaven to hell. We need not now discuss the cause of your failure; you were overtaken in some sudden temptation, or you neglected communion with God, or you refused to live up to your light. But the sad fact remains that you have failed, perhaps as Elijah did, when everyone expected you to stand. And you are ashamed. You want to hide yourself from all who knew you in happier days. You have given up heart and hope and lie dejected and dispirited on the desert sands; you account yourself forsaken by God and man. But remember, though forsaken by man, you are not forgotten of God. He loves you still, and pities you, and yearns over you; and waits beside you, with loving tendance and provender, in order to restore your soul, and give you back the years that the cankerworm and caterpillar have eaten. We have then, in this incident, four thoughts of the love of God which must be a comfort to us all and especially to those who have fallen from Carmel's height to the level of the desert sands.

God's Love in Its Constancy

It is a fact which we all admit, but which we seldom realize in the moments of depression and darkness to which we are all exposed. It is not difficult to believe that God loves us when we go with the multitude to the house of God, with the voice of joy and praise, and stand in the inner sunlit circle; but it is hard to believe that He feels as much love for us when, exiled by our sin to the land of Jordan and of the Hermonites, our soul is cast down within us, and deep calls to deep, as His waves and billows surge around. It is not difficult to believe that God loves us when, like Elijah at Cherith and on Carmel, we do His commandments, hearkening unto the voice of His word; but it is not so easy when, like Elijah in the desert, we lie stranded. It is not difficult to believe in God's love when with Peter we stand on the mount of glory and, in the rapture of joy, propose to share a tabernacle with Christ evermore; but it is nearly impossible when, with the same apostle, we deny our Master with oaths, and are abashed by a look in which grief masters reproach.

Yet we must learn to know and believe he constancy of the love of God. We may not feel it. We may deem it shut up and gone forever. We may imagine that we have forfeited all claim to it. We may think of it as Arctic travelers, dying in the icy darkness, dream of the summers of early childhood. But nevertheless, it has not altered. Staunch as the affection of a friend, true as the love of a mother, the love of God abides unchangeable as Himself. Mists, born of the swamps and marshes of your own sin, obscure the light of that sun; but it is shining yet as brilliantly as ever and will shine on until it has dispelled all shrouding veils and bathes you again in its warm and blessed glow.

O man of God, lying amid the wrecks of what might have been, take heart! Hope still in the love of God; trust in it; yield to it; and you shall yet praise Him who is the health of your countenance and your God.

God's Love Manifested in Special Tenderness Because of Special Sin

We do not read that an angel ever appeared to Elijah at Cherith or Zarephath or awakened him with a touch that must have been as thrilling as it was tender. Ravens and brooklets and a widow woman, had ministered to him before, but never an angel. He had drunk of the water of Cherith, but never of water drawn by angel hands from the river of God, which is ever full of water. He had eaten of bread and flesh foraged for him by ravens and of meal multiplied by miracle, but never of cakes molded by angel fingers. Why these special proofs of tenderness? Certainly it was not because God took any pleasure in His servant's sin or condoned his grave offense, but because a special manifestation of love was needed to convince the prophet that he was still dearly loved, to soften his spirit, and lead him to repentance.

Where ordinary methods will not avail, God will employ extraordinary ones. There is one memorable instance of this which has afforded comfort and hope to multitudes who have sinned as Peter did. This multitude will bless God forever for the record of the Master's dealings with His truant servant. The Lord sent a general message to all His disciples to meet Him in Galilee. But He felt that Peter would hardly dare to class himself with the rest, so Jesus sent to him a special message through an angel. "Tell his disciples, and Peter" (Mar_16:7). It is thus that Jesus is working still throughout the circles of His disciples. So eager is He to convince the fallen of his unaltered love, that He will go out of His way to show it. He will invent new and unwonted surprises. He will employ angels with their gentle touch and bake special cakes on desert stones. He will send special messages, entwined about the backslider's name. He will take the wondering sheep on His shoulder to bring it home. He will kill the fatted calf and call on the angels of His presence-chamber to make merry and be glad.

It may be that you are sleeping the sleep of insensibility or of despair, but all the while the love of God is inventing some unique manifestation of its yearning tenderness. He hates your sin as only infinite holiness can. He yearns over you as only infinite love can. He wants to convince you of what He feels; to touch you, to soften you, to win you back to Himself. All the while that you are grieving Him and wandering from Him, He is encompassing you with blessings. Be conquered! Yield to Him! Take with you words, and turn again to the Lord. He will receive you graciously.

God's Love in Its Unwearied Care

It is most likely that it was evening when the angel came the first time and touched him, and bade him arise and eat; for we are told that he went a day's journey into the wilderness before he sat down under the juniper bush. Night was spreading her temporary veil over the scorched sands, and the sun was sinking like a ball of fire on the unbroken rim of the horizon. And when the angel of the Lord came the second time, it would probably be as morning was breaking over the world. And thus, through the intervening night, the angels of God kept watch and ward about the sleeping prophet.

None of us can measure the powers of endurance of the love of God. It never tires. It fainteth not, neither is weary. It does not fail, nor is it discouraged. It bears all things, believes all things, hopes all things, endures all things. It clings about its object with a divine tenacity until the darkness and wanderings are succeeded by the blessedness of former days. It watches over us during the hours of our insensibility to its presence, touching us ever, speaking to us, and summoning us to arise to a nobler, better life, one more worthy of ourselves and more glorifying to Him.

70

God's Love Anticipating Coming Need

This always stands out as one of the most wonderful passages in the prophet's history. We can understand God giving him, instead of a long discourse, a good meal and sleep as the best means of recruiting his spent powers. This is what we should have expected of One who knows our frame and remembers that we are dust and who pities us as a father pities his children. But it is very wonderful that God should provision His servant for the long journey that lay before him, "Arise and eat, because the journey is too great for thee" (1Ki_19:7).

That journey was undertaken at his own whim. It was one long flight from his post of duty, it was destined to meet with a grave remonstrance at its close: "What doest thou here, Elijah?" (1Ki_19:9). And yet the Lord graciously gave him food, in the strength of which he could endure he long fatigue. The explanation must be again sought in the tender love of God. Elijah's nature was clearly overwrought. Without doubt he had steadfastly made up his mind for that tedious journey to the Mount of God. Nothing would turn him from his fixed purpose. And therefore, as he would go, God anticipated his needs, though they were the needs of a truant servant and a rebellious child. In wrath He remembered mercy, and provided him with the blessings of His goodness. God imparted, through a single meal, sufficient strength for a march of forty days and forty nights. Let us pause here for a moment to adore the wonderful love of God which gives men life and breath and all things, even when He knows that they will be used for selfish ends and in direct opposition to His revealed will.

Surely these thoughts of the love of God will arrest some from pursuing any longer the path of the backslider. You have failed, but do not be afraid of God or think that He will never look on you again. In thinking thus of Him, you grieve Him more and aggravate your bad behavior. Rather, cast yourself upon His love as a swimmer flings himself upon the buoyant waves which immediately close around him and bear him up and carry him upon their sunlit bosom. Tell Him how deeply you mourn the past. Ask Him to restore you. Give yourself to Him again, resume the forsaken work, retake the abandoned post. Believe hat God will again use you as a chosen vessel and pour through you His tides of blessing as an ocean may pour its flood through one narrow strait.

And as we close this precious narrative, may we all receive instruction concerning those meals which heaven prepares for us, each evening and morning, during our journey across the sands of time. At night, when we come home wearied with the day's toil, before we fling ourselves into deep slumber, the angels bid us arise and partake of that living bread and water on which alone can spirits become strong. And morning by morning their gentle touches awake us from overdue slumbers, as they whisper, "Arise and eat, lest the journey be too great for thee." their neglect to obey the heavenly summons is the true cause of so much failure in the lives of Christian people. They do not feed enough on Christ. They slumber on, heedless and insensate, until the morning sun is high, and the angels, with their provisions, have faded away.

May we be among the happy number who never need twice calling, but who rise each morning as the first cadence of the angel's voice breaks upon their ears, to eat of that flesh which is meat indeed, and to drink of the blood which is drink indeed. Then shall we be able to withstand all assaults, to endure all fatigue, and to abide perpetually in the realized presence of God. "They that wait upon the LORD shall renew their strength; they shall mount up with wings as eagles; they shall run, and not be weary; and they shall walk, and not faint" (Isa_40:31).

Chapter Twelve - The "Still Small Voice"

Refreshed by sleep and food, Elijah resumed his journey across the desert to Horeb. Perhaps no spot on earth is more associated with the manifested presence of God than that sacred mount. It was there the bush burned with fire, there the law was given, there Moses spent forty days and nights alone with God. It was a natural instinct that led the prophet thither, and all the world could not have furnished a more appropriate school. Natural scenery and holy associations lent all their powers to impress and elevate the soul.

Forty times the prophet saw the sun rise and set over the desert waste. I do not know that anyone has perfectly explained the meaning of that symbolic number which so frequently appears upon the page of Scripture, and is so often associated with failure and temptation. In passing, I can only note the fact of its frequent repetition. Thus, at last, the prophet came to Horeb, the mount of God. We have to consider how God dealt with His dispirited and truant child.

God Spoke to Him

In some dark cave, among those rent precipices Elijah lodged, and, as he waited in lonely musings, the fire burned in his soul. But he had not long to wait. "Behold, the word of the LORD came unto him (1Ki_19:9).

That word had often come to him before. It had come to him at Thisbe. It had come to him in Samaria, after he had given his first message to Ahab. It had come to him when Cherith was dry. It had come to summon him from the solitudes of Zarephath to the stir of active life. And now it found him out and came to him again. There is no spot on earth so lonely, no cave so deep and dark, that the word of the Lord cannot discover and come to us.

But though God had often spoken to him before, He had never spoken in quite the same tone -- "What doest thou here. Elijah?" (1Ki_19:1-21; 1Ki_13:1-34). The accent was stern and reproachful, and seemed to mean, "Thou art My servant; thou art set to do My will; if ever thou wast needed, it is now; the tide is on the turn; a great reformation is almost ripe. Why hast thou left thy post? How camest thou hither without My bidding or My leave?" Elijah shrank from a direct reply. If he had answered truly, he must have confessed that he was utterly in the wrong, without a single word of extenuation or excuse. He had done wrong in leaving his post; and that first wrong step had been aggravated by every one which he had taken since, plunging him further and further into the dark.

If the prophet had answered that searching question of God with shame and sorrow, if he had confessed that he had failed and asked for forgiveness, if he had cast himself on the pitifulness and tenderness of his Almighty Friend -- there is not the least doubt that he would have been forgiven and restored. The past would never have been named against him, and the results of his fatal flight would have been repaired. God would Himself have stood in the breach, until His child could hasten back again to his post and lead on the glorious work which he had so nobly commenced. But instead of this, he parried the divine question and evaded it. He did not try to explain how he came there, or what he was doing. He chose rather to dwell upon his own loyalty for the cause of God and to bring it out into striking relief by contrasting it with the sinful backslidings of his people. "I have been very jealous for the LORD God of hosts: for the children of Israel have forsaken thy covenants, thrown down thine altars, and slain thy prophets with the sword; and I, even I only, am left; and they seek my life, to take it away" (1Ki_19:10). All this was well known to God, and I do not think the prophet would ever have alluded to it unless he had been hard pressed to find an excuse to palliate his own cowardice and neglect of duty.

In fact, he was thoroughly demoralized with unbelief and fear. The sky of his soul was covered with clouds so dense that no star of comfort glimmered through their murky curtains. There was a tinge of self-vindication and of blame on others, which was scarcely worthy of him. He did not sufficiently realize that the fault lay with himself and that he, equally with others, was to blame for the pass to which the cause of God had come. His was a noble nature under a temporary cloud, a palace in ruins, a splendid vessel rolling rudderless in the trough of the waves. There was, no doubt, truth in what he said. He was full of zeal and holy devotion to the cause of God. He had often mourned over the national degeneracy. He keenly felt his own isolation and loneliness. But these were not the reasons why at the moment he was hiding in the cave, nor were they the real answer to that searching question, "What doest thou here, Elijah?"

How often is that question put still! When a Christian worker, to avoid some difficulty or to secure selfish gratification and ease, deserts his post and escapes to that couch of indolence or that forest glade where soft breezes blow, the question comes, "What doest thou here?" When a child of God is found in the theater, the dancing saloon, or the place of evil companionship, sitting in the seat of scorners, or walking in the way of the ungodly, again must the question come as a thunderbolt out of a clear sky, "What doest thou here?" When one endowed with great faculties digs a hole in the earth and buries the God- entrusted talent, standing idle all the day long among the loungers in the marketplace, again the inquiry must ring out, "What doest thou here?"

Life is the time for doing. The world is a great workshop, in which there is no room for drones. God Himself worketh as the great Master builder. All creatures fulfill their needful functions, from the angel that hymns God's praise to the wasp that buries a corpse. There is plenty to do -- evil to put down; good to build up; doubters to be directed; prodigals to be won back; sinners to be sought. "What doest thou here?" Up, Christians, leave your caves, and do! Do not do in order to be saved; but being saved, do!

God Taught Him by A Beautiful, Natural Parable

He was bidden to stand at the entrance to the cave; but this he hesitated to do until afterward. Did that hesitancy arise from a guilty conscience, reminding him that all was not right between him and God?

Presently there was the sound of the rushing of a mighty wind, and in another moment a violent tornado was sweeping past. Nothing could withstand its fury. It rent the mountains, and broke in pieces the rocks before the Lord. The valleys were littered with splintered fragments; but

74

the Lord was not in the wind. And when the wind had died away, there was an earthquake. The mountain swayed to and fro, yawning and crack-ing. The ground heaved as if an Almighty hand were passing beneath it, but the Lord was not in the earthquake. And when the earthquake was over, there was a fire. The heavens were one blaze of light, each pinnacle and peak glowed in the kindling flame. The valley beneath looked like a huge smelting- furnace, but the Lord was not in the fire.

How strange! Surely these were the appropriate natural symbols of the divine presence. If we had been asked to describe it, we should have used these first of all. But hark! A still small whisper is in the air -- very still, and very small, like the trembling echoes of a flute which is being played among the hills. It touched the listening heart of the prophet. If the more tumultuous outburst of power had expressed the storm and tumult of his nature, this elicited and interpreted a sweeter, nobler self, and cast a softening spell over his tempest-tossed spirit, and seemed to be the tender cadence of the love and pity of God which had come in search of him. Its music drew him from the cave, into the innermost re-cesses of which he had been driven by the terrible convulsions of nature. "And it was so, when Elijah heard it, that he wrapped his face in his man-tle, and went out, and stood in the entering in of the cave" (1Ki_19:13).

What was the meaning of all this? It is not difficult to understand. Eli-jah was most eager that his people should be restored to their allegiance to God, and he thought that it could only be done by some striking and wonderful act. He may have often spoken thus with himself: "Those idols shall never be swept from our land, unless God sends a movement swift and irresistible as the wind, which hurries the clouds before it. The land can never be awakened except by a moral earthquake. There must be a baptism of fire." And when he stood on Carmel and beheld the panic among the priests and the eagerness among the people, he thought that the time -- the set time -- had come. But all that died away. That was not God's chosen way of saving Israel. And because He did not go on working thus, Elijah thought that He was not working at all, and he abandoned himself to the depths of despondency.

But in this natural parable, God seemed to say, "My child, thou hast been looking for Me to answer thy prayers with striking signs and won-ders; and because these have not been given in a marked and permanent form, thou hast thought Me heedless and inactive. But I am not always to be found in these great visible movements. I love to work gently, softly, and unperceived. I have been working so, and I am working so still. There are in Israel, as the results of My quiet, gentle ministry, seven thousand, all the knees which have not bowed unto Baal, and every mouth which hath not kissed him." Yes, and was not the gentle ministry of Elisha, which succeeded the stormy career of his great predecessor like the still small voice after the wind, the earthquake, and the fire? And is it not probably that more real good was effected by his unobtrusive life and miracles, than was even wrought by the splendid deeds of Elijah?

We often fall into similar mistakes. When we wish to promote a revival, we seek to secure large crowds, much evident impression, powerful preachers; influences comparable to the wind, the earthquake, and the fire. When these are present, we account that we are secure of having the presence and power of God. But surely nature itself rebukes us. Who hears the roll of the planets? Who can detect the falling of the dew? Whose eye has ever been injured by the breaking of the wavelets of daylight on the shores of our planet? At this moment the mightiest forces are in operation around us, but there is nothing to betray their presence. And thus it was with the ministry of the Lord Jesus. He did not strive, nor cry, nor lift up nor cause His voice to be heard in the streets. While men were expecting Him at the front door with blare of trumpet, He stepped into His destined home in the disguise of a peasant's child. His going forth is ever prepared as the morning. He comes down as showers on the mown grass. His Spirit descends as the dove, whose wings make no tremor in the still air. Let us take heart! God may not be working as we expect, but He is working. If not in the wind, yet in the zephyr. If not in the earthquake, yet in the heartbreak. If not in the fire, yet in the warmth of summer. If not in thunder, yet in the still small voice. If not in crowds, yet in lonely hearts, in silent tears, in the broken sobs of penitents, and in multitudes, who, like the seven thousand of Israel, are unknown as disciples.

But Elijah refused to be comforted. It seemed as if he could not shake off the mood in which he was ensnared. And so when God asked him the second time, "What doest thou here, Elijah?" (1Ki_19:13) he answered in the words with which he had tried to justify himself before: "And he said, I have been very jealous -- " (1Ki_19:14).

It is pleasant to think of those seven thousand disciples, known only to God. We are sometimes sad as we compare the scanty number of professing Christians with the masses of ungodly. But we may take heart, there are other Christians besides. That seemingly harsh governor is Joseph in disguise. That wealthy owner of the garden in Arimathea is a lowly follower of Jesus. That member of the Sanhedrin is a disciple, but secretly, for fear of the Jews. For every one entered on our rolls of communicants, there are hundreds -- perhaps thousands -- whom God shall reckon as His when He makes up His jewels. But if you are one of that number, I entreat you, do not remain so. It puts you in a false position, it robs the cause of God of your help and influence, it is an act of treachery to Christ Himself. Beware lest, if you are ashamed of Him, the time may come when He shall be ashamed of you.

It is quite true that confession means martyrdom in one form or another. Sometimes our heart and flesh shrink back in unutterable anguish as we contemplate the possible results of refusing the act of obeisance to Baal. But, at such times, let us cheer ourselves by anticipating the august moment when the dear Master will speak our names before assembled worlds and own us as His. And let us also ask Him in us and through us to speak out and witness a good confession, effecting that in us and by us which we are totally powerless to effect by ourselves.

We are all doing more good than we know. Elijah thought that he was doing nothing except when battling with idolatry and sin. He never thought how often he was helping those seven thousand by the indirect influence of his example. We, perhaps, accomplish less by our great efforts than we effect by a consistent life, a holy character, a daily shining. Lighthouse keepers never know how many weary, longing eyes turn in the darkness to the silent light that is maintained through the dark night. Our duty is to shine, not asking questions, not eager for great results; but content to do the will of God, consistently, humbly, and constantly, sure that God is not unrighteous to forget our work of faith and labor of love.

Chapter Thirteen - "Go, Return!"

It is a very solemn thought that one sin may forever, so far as this world is concerned, wreck our usefulness. It is not always so. Sometimes -- as in the case of the apostle Peter -- the Lord graciously restores and recommissions for His work the one who might have been counted unfit ever again to engage in it. "Feed my sheep. Feed my lambs." But against this one case we may put three others, in each of which it would seem as if the sentry angel, who forbade the return of our first parents to Eden, were stationed with strict injunctions to forbid any return to the former position of noble service.

The first case is that of Moses. No other man has ever been honored as was he, "with whom God spake face to face" -- the meekest of men, the servant of the Lord, the foster-nurse of the Jewish nation, whose intercessions saved them again and again from destruction. Yet, because he spake unadvised with his lips and smote the rock twice in unbelief and passion, he was compelled to bear the awful sentence, "Because ye believed me not, to sanctify me in the eyes of the children of Israel, therefore ye shall not bring this congregation into the land which I have given them! (Num_20:12). Most earnestly did he plead for a revocation of that terrible prohibition. But he was silenced by the solemn reply, against which there was no appeal, "Let it suffice thee; speak no more unto me of this matter" (Deu_3:26).

The second case is that of Saul, the first, ill-fated king of Israel whose reign opened so auspiciously, as a morning without clouds; but who soon brought upon himself the sentence of deposition. Yet it was only for a single act. Alarmed at Samuel's long delay and at the scattering of the people, he intruded rashly into a province from which he was expressly excluded and offered the sacrifice with which the Israelites were wont to prepare for battle. "And it came to pass, that as soon as he had made an end of offering the burnt-offering, behold, Samuel came... And Samuel said, What hast thou done?... Thou hast done foolishly; thou hast not kept the commandment of the LORD thy God, which he commanded thee: for now would the LORD have established thy kingdom upon Israel forever. But now thy kingdom shall not continue;... because thou hast not kept that which the LORD commanded thee" (1Sa_13:10-14). Early in his reign and before his further disobedience in the case of the Amalekites -- for that one act of disobedience, revealing, as it did, a sad state of moral decrepitude -- Saul was rejected.

The third case is that of Elijah. He was never reinstated in quite the position which he had occupied before his fatal flight. True, he was bidden to return on his way, and work was indicated for him to do. But that work was the anointing of three men who were to share among them the ministry which he might have fulfilled if only he had been true to his opportunities and faithful to his God. God's work must go on; if not by us, then, through our failures, by others brought in to supply our place. "Go, return on thy way to the wilderness of Damascus: and when thou comest, anoint Hazael to be king over Syria; and Jehu the son of Nimshi shalt thou anoint to be king over Israel; and Elisha the son of Shaphat of Abelmeholah shalt thou anoint to be prophet in thy room." Those words rang out the death knell of Elijah's fondest dreams. Evidently, it was not for him to be the deliverer of his people from the thralldom of Baal. Others were to do his work; another was to be prophet in his room.

All those who hold prominent positions as teachers and leaders may well take warning by these solemn examples standing on the plains of time, as Lot's wife on those of Sodom. We may not all be tempted, as Elijah was, to unbelief and discouragement. But there are many other snares prepared for us by our great enemy and strewn over with fair appearances, as the hunter strews earth and grass on the top of the pitfall which he has dug in the pathway between the river and the lair of his prey. There is the adulation given to the successful man in which so much of the human is mingled with thankfulness for the help or comfort given. There is the desire to be always prominent -- foremost on every platform and first in every enterprise -- to the utter neglect of private prayer. There are the insidious attacks of jealousy, depreciation of others, comparison of their standing with our own. And in addition to these are other modes of failure, more gross and evident than they, to which we are all prone, and by which, alas! too many have been mastered. Any one of these may compel God to cast us away from His glorious service and employs us in a humbler ministry, or to anoint our successors.

As children, He will never cast us away; but as His servants He may. Let us beware! One false step, one hurried desertion of our post, one act of disobedience, one outburst of passion; any one of these may lead our heavenly Father to throw us aside, as Samson did the jawbone of the ass with which he had slain heaps upon heaps. We shall not forfeit heaven; that is guaranteed to us by the precious blood of Christ. We may even be favored by a glorious and triumphant entrance thither in an equipage of flame. But we shall never again ride on the crest of the flowing tide, carrying all before us. Others shall finish our uncompleted task.

But with the danger there are sufficient safeguards. Let God prune you with the golden pruning-knife of His holy Word. Look into the mirror of revealed truth, to see if there is any trace of blemish stealing over the face of the soul. Offer your spirit constantly to the Holy Spirit, that He may detect and reveal to you the beginnings of the sin of idolatry. Be very jealous of anything that divides your heart with your Lord. "Watch and pray, lest ye enter into temptation" (Mar_14:38). Have perpetual recourse for cleansing, to the blood shed for the remission of sin. Trust in Him who is able to guard you from stumbling, and to set you before the presence of His glory without blemish, in exceeding joy.

But now, turning to the further study of the words with which God dismissed His servant from Horeb, let us notice three distinct thoughts.

The Variety of God's Instruments

Hazael, king of Syria; Jehu, the rude captain; and Elisha, the young farmer. Each was as different as possible from the others, and yet each was needed for some special work in connection with that idolatrous people. Hazael was destined to be the rod of divine vengeance to Israel at large, by whom God began to cut them short, and to make them like the dust by threshing. Ah! cruel indeed was his treatment of them! (2Ki_5:12;

2Ki_10:32; 2Ki_12:3, 2Ki_12:17). Jehu was to be the scourge of the house of Ahab, extirpating it root and branch. Elisha's ministry was to be genial and gentle as summer rain and evening dew, like the ministry of our Lord Himself whom Elisha prefigured and of whom his name significantly spoke.

It is remarkable how God accomplishes His purposes through men who only think of working their own wild way. Their sin is not diminished or condoned because they are executing the designs of heaven, it still stands out in all its malignant deformity. And yet, though they are held accountable for the evil, it is nonetheless evident that they do whatsoever God's hand and God's counsel determined before to be done. This fact is often referred to in Scripture. Joseph comforted his brethren after his father's death, by telling them that though they thought evil against him, God meant it for good, to save people. David forbade his men to slay Shimei because, though Shimei cursed David, and cursing the king was a foul act of treason, yet "the LORD hath said unto him, Curse David" (2Sa_16:10). And our blessed Lord, when about to be delivered into the hands of wicked men, said that His Father was putting the cup into His hands (see Act_2:23).

Men may do evil things against us for which they will be condemned, and yet those very things, being permitted by the wisdom and love of God, are His messages to us. Before they can reach us, they must pass through His environing, encompassing presence. If they do, then they are God's will for us, and we must meekly accept our Father's plan, saying, "Not my will, but Thine be done."

No One Can Entirely Escape from God's Personal Dealings

God's nets are not all constructed with the same meshes. Men may escape through some of them; but they cannot escape through all. If they elude the Gospel ministry, they will be caught by some earnest worker, apt at personal dealing. If they manage to evade all contact with the living voice, they may yet be reached by the printed page. If they evade all religious literature, they may still be the sudden subjects of the strivings of the Spirit. "Him that escapeth the sword of Hazael shall Jehu slay: and him that escapeth from the sword of Jehu shall Elisha slay" (1Ki_19:17).

We do not read that Elisha ever wielded the sword, and yet the ministry of gentle love is sometimes more potent in slaying souls than the more vigorous ministry of an Hazael or Jehu; and out of such slaying comes life.

Let us not compare man with man. Let us not despise any sect or denomination or body of Christian workers. What is inoperative with one is God's voice to another. We are totally unable to estimate the essential use of men. And let us not envy one another, because each of us has some special gift which qualifies us for the use of the dear Master and enables us to touch some who would be unreached if it were not for us. "But now are they many members, yet but one body. And the eye cannot say unto the hand, I have no need of thee; nor again the head to the feet, I have no need of you" (1Co_12:21).

And as we look around on the entire range of ministry by which the world is filled, we may be sure that everyone has at least one chance, and that God so orders the lives of men that once at least during their course they are encountered by the kind of argument which is most appropriate to their character and temperament, if only they will give ear and yield.

God Never Overlooks One of His Own

Elijah thought that he alone was left as a lover and worshiper of God. It was a great mistake. God had Many hidden ones: "Yet I have left me seven thousand in Israel, all the knees which have not bowed unto Baal, and every mouth which hath not kissed him" (1Ki_19:18). We know nothing of their names or history. They were probably unknown in camp or court; obscure, simple-hearted, and humble. Their only testimony was one long refusal to the solicitations of the foul rites of idolatry. They groaned and wept in secret and spake often one to another, while the Lord hearkened and heard. But they were all known to God and enrolled among His jewels and counted as a shepherd tells his sheep. He cared for them with an infinite solicitude, and it was for their sake that He raised up the good and gentle Elisha to carry on the nurture and discipline of their souls.

It has often been a subject of wonder to me how these seven thousand secret disciples could keep so close as to be unknown by their great leader. Attar of a rose will always betray its presence, hide it as we may. When salt has not lost its savor, it cannot be hid. And the work of God in human hearts must, sooner or later, discover itself. It is to be feared, therefore, that the godliness of these hidden ones was very vague and colorless, needing the eye of omniscience to detect it. But for all that, God did detect it, and He prized it. He did not quench the smoking flax, but fanned it. He did not despise the grain of mustard seed, He watched its growth with tender love and care.

You may be very weak and insignificant -- not counted in the numberings of God's captains, nor deemed worthy of a name or place among His avowed servants. Yet if you have but a spark of faith and love, if you strive to keep yourself untainted by the world, you will be owned by Him whose scepter is stretched out to the most timid suppliant. But remember, if your inner life be genuine, it will not remain forever secret. It will break out as a long hidden fire; it will force its way into the light as the buried seed in which there is the spark of life.

It may be that God, by these lines, will speak to some backslider, saying: Go, return! Return to Me, from whom you have wandered. Return to My work, which you have deserted. Return to the posture of faith, from which you have fallen. Return to the happy, holy childlikeness of former years. "Return, ye backsliding children, and I will heal your backslidings" (Jer_3:22). Oh that the response may be, "Behold, we come unto thee; for thou art the LORD our God" (Jer_3:22).

Chapter Fourteen - Naboth's Vineyard

In a room of the palace, Ahab, king of Israel, lies upon his couch with his face toward the wall, refusing to eat. What has taken place? Has disaster befallen the royal arms? Have the priests of Baal been again massacred? Is his royal consort dead? No, the soldiers are still flushed with their recent victories over Syria. The worship of Baal has quite recovered the terrible disaster of Carmel. Jezebel -- resolute, crafty, cruel, and beautiful -- is now standing by his side, anxiously seeking the cause of this sadness which was, perhaps, assumed to engage her sympathy and to secure through her means, ends which he dared not compass for himself.

The story is soon told. Jezreel was the Windsor of Israel and the location of the favorite royal house. On a certain occasion, while Ahab was engaged there in superintending his large and beautiful pleasure-grounds, his eye lighted on a neighboring vineyard which belonged to Naboth the Jezreelite. It promised to be so valuable an addition to his property, that he resolved to procure it at all hazards. He therefore sent for Naboth and offered a better vineyard in exchange or the worth of it in money. To his surprise and indignation, Naboth refused both. And Naboth said to Ahab, "The LORD forbid it be, that I should give the inheritance of my fathers unto thee" (1Ki_21:3).

At first sight this refusal seems churlish and discourteous. But a little consideration will justify the refusal of Naboth, and aggravate the subsequent guilt of the royal pair. By the law of Moses, Canaan was considered as being, in a peculiar sense, God's land. The Israelites were His tenants, and one of the conditions of their tenure was that they should not alienate that which fell to their lot except in cases of extreme necessity, and then only until the year of Jubilee. The transfer was always coupled with the condition that the land might be redeemed at any moment before that time by the payment of a stipulated price. If these two conditions had remained in force, Naboth would have felt less compunction at this temporary alienation of his paternal inheritance; but both had probably fallen into disuse, and he anticipated that if it once passed out of his hands, his patrimony would become merged in the royal demesne, never to be disintegrated. Taking his stand then on religious grounds, he might well say, "The LORD forbid it me." His refusal was in part, therefore, a religious act.

But there was, without doubt, something further. In his mention of "the inheritance of his fathers," we have the suggestion of another, and most natural, reason for his reluctance. Beneath those vines and trees his fathers had for generations sat. There he had spent the sunny years of childhood. Many a holy memory was associated with that spot, and he felt that all the juice ever pressed from all the vineyards in the neighborhood would never compensate him for the wrench from those clustered memories.

Naboth's refusal made Ahab leap into his chariot and drive back to Samaria and, like a spoiled child, turn his face to the wall in a pet, "heavy and displeased." At the close of the previous chapter we learn that he was heavy and displeased with God; now he is agitated by the same strong passions toward man. In a few more days the horrid deed of murder was perpetrated, which at one stroke removed Naboth, his sons, and his heirs and the unclaimed property fell naturally into royal hands. There are many lessons here which would claim our notice if we were dealing with the whole story, but we must pass them by to bend our attention exclusively on the part Elijah played amid these terrible transactions.

He Was Called Back to Service

How many years had elapsed since last the word of the Lord had come to Elijah, we do not know. Perhaps it was five or six. All this while he must have waited wistfully for the well-known accents of that voice, longing to hear it once again. And the weary days, passing slowly by, prolonged his deferred hope into deep and yet deeper regret, he must have been driven to continued soul- questionings and heart-searchings, to bitter repentance for the past, and to renewed consecration for whatever service might be imposed upon him. Using a phrase employed of Samson who was as remarkable for physical force as Elijah was for spiritual power, we may say, "the hair of his head began to grow again."

It may be that these words will be read by some, once prominent in the Christian service, who have been lately cast aside. They have been removed from the sphere they once filled. They have found audiences slip away from them, and opportunities close up. They have seen younger people step in to fill the ranks from which they have fallen. This may be attributable to the sovereignty of the Great Master, who has a perfect right to do as He will with His own, and who takes up one and lays down another. But before we lay this flattering unction to our souls, we should inquire whether the reason may not lie within our own breasts, in some inconsistency or sin which needs confession and forgiveness at the hands of our faithful and merciful High Priest, before ever again the word of the Lord can come to us.

It is also quite possible that we are left unused for our own deeper teaching in the ways of God. Hours, even years of silence are full of golden opportunities for the servants of God. In such cases, our conscience does not condemn us or accost us with any sufficient reason arising from ourselves. Our simple duty is to keep clean and filled and ready, standing on the shelf, meet for the Master's use, sure that we serve if we only stand and wait and knowing that He will accept and reward the willingness for the deed.

Elijah Was Not Disobedient

Once before, when his presence was urgently required, he had arisen to flee for his life. But there was no vacillation, no cowardice now. His old heroic faith had revived in him again. His spirit had regained its wonted posture in the presence of Jehovah. His nature had returned to its equipoise in the will of God. He arose and went down to the vineyard of Naboth and entered it and strode through its glades, or waited at the gates, to find the royal criminal. It was nothing to him that there rode behind Ahab's chariot two ruthless captains, Jehu and Bidkar (2Ki_9:25). He did not for a moment consider that the woman who had threatened his life before might now take it, maddened as she was with her recent draught of human blood. All fear was but as the cobweb swinging across the garden pathway and swept before the child rushing resolutely forward. Who does not rejoice that Elijah had such an opportunity of wiping out the dark stain of disgrace which attached to him from the moment when he had forsaken, so faithlessly, the post of duty? His time of waiting had not been lost on him!

He Was Acting as An Incarnate Conscience

Naboth was out of the way, and Ahab may have comforted himself, as weak people do still, with the idea that he was not his murderer. How could he be? He had been perfectly quiescent. He had simply put his face to the wall and done nothing. He did remember that Jezebel had asked him for his royal seal to give validity to some letters which she had written in his name, but how was he to know what she had written? Of course if she had given instructions for Naboth's death it was a great pity, but it could not now be helped. He might as well take possession of the inheritance! With such palliatives he succeeded in stilling the fragment of conscience which alone survived in his heart. And it was then that he was startled by a voice which he had not heard for years, saying, "Thus says the LORD, Hast thou killed, and also taken possession?" (1Ki_21:19). He killed! No, it was Jezebel that had killed. Ah, it was in vain to shift the responsibility thus! "Hast thou killed?" The prophet, guided by the Spirit of God, put the burden on the right shoulders.

Often a man, who dares not to do a disgraceful act himself will call a subordinate to his side and say: "Such a thing needs doing, I wish you would see to it. Use any of my appliances you will, only do not trouble me further about it -- and of course you had better not do anything wrong." In God's sight that man is held responsible for whatever evil is done by his tool in the execution of this commission. The blame is laid on the shoulders of the principal; and it will be more tolerable for the subordinate than for him, in the day of Judgment.

Further than that but based on the same principle; if an employer, by paying an inadequate and unjust wage, tempts his employees to supplement their scanty pittance by dishonest or unholy methods, he is held responsible in the sight of heaven for the evil which he might have prevented if he had not been willfully and criminally indifferent.

It is sometimes the duty of a servant of God fearlessly to rebuke sinners who think their high position a license to evildoing and a screen from rebuke. And let all such remember that acts of high-handed sin often seem at first to prosper. Naboth meekly dies, the earth sucks in his blood, the vineyard passes into the oppressor's hands, but there is One who sees and will most certainly avenge the cause of His servants. "Surely I have seen yesterday the blood of Naboth, and the blood of his sons, saith the LORD; and I will requite thee in this plat" (2Ki_9:26). That vengeance may tarry, for the mills of God grind slowly; but it will come as certainly as God is God. And in the meanwhile, in Naboth's vineyard stands Elijah the prophet; and in the criminal's heart stands conscience with its scourge of small cords, weighted with jagged metal. This lesson is enforced again and again by our great dramatist, who teaches men who will not read their Bibles that sin does not pay in the end. No matter how successful it may seem at first, in the end it has to reckon with an Elijah as conscience, and he always finds out the culprit; and with God as an avenger -- and He never misses His mark.

He Was Hated for The Truth's Sake

"And Ahab said to Elijah, Hast thou found me, O mine enemy?" (1Ki_21:20). Though the king knew it not, Elijah was his best friend, while it was Jezebel who was his direst foe. But sin distorts everything. It is like the gray dawn which so obscures the most familiar objects that men mistake friends for foes and foes for friends. Many a time have men repeated the error of the disciples, who mistook Jesus for an evil spirit and cried out for fear.

When Christian friends remonstrate with evil-doers, rebuke their sins, and warn them of their doom, the Christians are scouted, hated, and denounced as enemies. The Bible is detested because it so clearly exposes sin and its consequences. God Himself is viewed with dislike. It cannot be otherwise. The Egyptians hated the blessed pillar of cloud. The Philistines sent away the ark of the covenant. Wounds shrink from salt. The broken bone dreads the gentle touch of the physician. The thief hates the detective's lantern.

Let us not be surprised if we are hated. Let us even be thankful when men detest us -- not for ourselves, but for the truths we speak. Let us "rejoice, and be exceeding glad." When bad men think thus of us, it is an indication that our influence is at the very antipodes to the bent and tenor of their lives. "Blessed are ye, when men shall revile you, and persecute you, and shall say all manner of evil against you falsely, for my sake. Rejoice, and be exceeding glad; for great is your reward in heaven: for so persecuted they the prophets which were before you" (Mat_5:11-12).

Oh, do not turn from the surgeon's knife, or the lighthouse gleam, or the red warning light, or the deep baying of the hound -- as if these were your foes. It is you that is wrong; not they.

He Was a True Prophet

Each of the woes which Elijah foretold came true. Ahab postponed their fulfillment for some three years by a partial repentance, but at the end of that time he went back to his evil ways, and every item was literally fulfilled. He was wounded by a chance arrow at Ramoth-gilead, "and the blood ran out of the wound into the midst of the chariot" (1Ki_22:35) and as they washed his chariot in the fountain of Samaria, the dogs licked his blood. Twenty years after, when Jehu sent out to see, there was nothing of Jezebel left for burial. Only her skull, feet, and palms, escaped the voracious dogs as she lay exposed on that very spot. The corpse of their son Joram was cast forth unburied on that same plot, at the command of Jehu, who never forgot those memorable words. And there, in after days, the armies of Israel were put again and again to the rout, saturating the soil with richer fluid than ever flowed from the crushed grapes of the vine. God is true, not only to His promises, but to His threats.

Every word spoken by Elijah was literally fulfilled. Jehovah put His own seal upon His servant's words. The passing years amply vindicated him. And as we close this tragic episode in has career, we rejoice to learn that he was reinstated in the favor of God and stamped again with the divine imprimatur of trustworthiness and truth.

Chapter Fifteen - The Old Courage Again

In order to understand the striking episode before us, we must think ourselves out of this dispensation, the main characteristic of which is gentle mercy, and imagine ourselves back in the age that ended at Calvary. It is very important to have a right understanding of our times. We must not judge the past ages by our own high standards of forgiveness and love, learned in the life and death of Jesus Christ, who is the last and supreme revelation of God. And we must not import into our own age methods of thought and action which were once permissible and necessary, because cognate to the spirit of their times.

This lesson was once impressively taught by our Lord to His disciples. Fresh from the transfiguration, He was on His way to the cross. For some reason He did not take the usual route along the eastern bank of the Jordan, but chose the more direct course through Samaria. Traveling thus, they had probably reached the spot, of which we are soon to speak, which was once scorched and blackened by the cinders of Ahaziah's troops. Below them, in the ravine, lay a village, to which they sent a deputation, asking for entertainment in the night, which was darkening over them. But religious bigotry triumphed over natural feeling, and the request was absolutely refused. Oh, if they had known that He was about to purchase the redemption of a world and institute a religion in which there should be neither Samaritan nor Jew, but one great brotherhood in Himself -- they would surely have bade Him welcome and pressed Him with hospitality, even though the mighty transaction was to take place within the limits of their hated rival, Jerusalem! "And when his disciples James and John saw this, they said, Lord, wilt thou that we command fire to come down from heaven, and consume them, even as Elias did? But He turned, and rebuked them, and said, Ye know not what manner of spirit ye are of" (Luk_9:54). It was as if He had said, "Remember that in Me you have passed into a new epoch; the affairs of the kingdom of heaven will be managed on altogether different lines from those with which you are familiar. I shall not destroy the law and the prophets; but I am introducing a code which shall fulfill them after a new fashion. The new regime of mercy is already begun."

Let us clearly define to ourselves the difference in the dispensations. This is after the Spirit of the Son, dwelling in the bosom of the Father; that was after the spirit of the servant, clad in ardent zeal for the glory of God. This glows with the lambent fire of the Holy Ghost; that with the devouring fire of destruction. The keynote of this is salvation; of that, vindication. The Old Testament brims with striking teaching of the holiness and righteousness of God. God, our Father, was as merciful and long suffering then as now; and He gave many sweet glimpses of His loving heart. These glimpses became more numerous as the ages brought nigh the incarnation of the love of God. But men cannot take in too many thoughts at once. Line must be on line, precept on precept. And so each preliminary age had some one special truth to teach, and that truth was accentuated and brought into prominence by special proofs and episodes. The age of the Mosaic Law, which shed its empire over the times of Elijah, was preeminently the era in which those awful and splendid attributes of the divine character -- God's holiness, justice, righteousness, and severity against sin -- stood out in massive prominence; as some of us have seen from the ancient capital of Switzerland, the long line of Bernese Alps rising above the plain in distant and majestic splendor, cold in the gray dawn or flushed with the light of morn and eve. It was only when those lessons had been completely learned that mankind was able to appreciate the love of God which is in Jesus Christ our Lord.

Critics -- who insensible have caught their conceptions of infinite love from the Gospels which they affect to despise -- find fault with the Old Testament because of its austere tones and its severe enactments. They point out many things inconsistent with the gentler spirit of our times. There is nothing surprising here. It could not have been otherwise in a gradual unfolding of the nature and character of God. The holy men who lived in those days had never heard the gentle voice of the Son of Man speaking the Sermon on the Mount. They had, however, very definite conceptions of the righteousness and holiness of God, and His swift indignation on sin. This inspired many of the Psalms in the hymnal of the Old Testament saints. This stimulated them to do deeds from which our gentler nature shrinks. But for this, Levi had never slain his brethren, or Joshua the Canaanites, Samuel had never hewed Agag in pieces before the Lord, and Elijah had never presumed to slay the priests of Baal or call down fire from heaven to destroy the captains and their men.

And, as we read these deeds, we may well sink into quiet self-questioning. We need not fall into the extreme of Cromwell and his soldiers and introduce the speech or acts of those bygone days into our dealings with the enemies of truth and God. But we do well to ask whether -- granting that we forego the outward manifestation -- there is the same hatred of sin, the same zeal for the glory of God, the same inveterate enthusiasm for righteousness as there was in those days of force and decision and unswerving righteousness.

These considerations will help us to understand the narrative that awaits us, and will relieve the character of Elijah from the charge of vindictiveness and passion. Then we can consider, without compunction, the rising up again in his breast of something of his old undaunted courage and heroic bearing.

The story is as follows: Ahaziah, the son of Ahab, had succeeded to his father's throne and his father's sins. He shrank in cowardly fear from the hardihood of the camp and the dangers of the field, leaving Moab to rebel without attempting its re-subjugation. He led a self-indulgent life in his palace. But the shafts of death can find us equally in apparent security as amid threatening dangers. He was leaning on the balustrade that fence the flat roof of the palace when it suddenly gave way, and he overbalanced himself and was flung to the ground. Many are the balustrades on which we lean in hours of peril, which fail us to our hurt! When the first panic was over, the king was seized with intense longings to know how his illness would turn. In a strange freak, he sent messengers to one of the ancient shrines of Canaan, which was dedicated to Baalzebub, the god of flies and the patron saint of medicine, who had some affinity with the Baal of his parents. This was a deliberate rejection of Jehovah, a daring choice of those ways which had brought the wrath of God on his father's house. It could not pass unnoticed, and Elijah was sent to meet his messengers as they were speeding across the plain of Esdraelon, with the announcement of certain death: "Thus saith the LORD... thou shalt not come down from that bed on which thou art gone up, but shalt surely die" (2Ki_1:16).

The servants did not know the stranger. They may have been imported Tyrians who had never mingled in the life of the nation, and who were ignorant of the mighty prophet of God. Years also had probably elapsed since his last public appearance. However, they were so impressed by that commanding figure and authoritative tone and so awed by that terrible reply, that they determined to return at once to the king. They found him lying on the divan covered with cushions, to which he had been carried from the scene of his accident. And they told him the reason of their speedy return. Ahaziah must have guessed who the man was that had dared to cross their path and send him such a message. But, to make assurance surer, he asked them to describe the mysterious stranger. They replied that he was a man of hair. Long and heavy tresses of unshorn hair hung heavily down upon his shoulders, his beard covered his breast and mingled with the unwrought skins that formed his only dress. It was enough. The king recognized him at once, and said, "It is Elijah the Tishbite."

Two emotions now filled his heart. He wanted, in exasperation, to get Elijah in his power to vent his wrath on him. He also, perhaps, cherished a secret hope that the lips which had announced his death might be induced to revoke it. He therefore resolved to capture him. For that purpose he sent a captain and a troop of fifty soldiers. When they were struck down in death, he sent another captain and his band. These men exceeded their duty. Instead of simply acting as the tools and instruments of the royal will, they spoke with an unwarrantable insolence, "Thou man of God, the king hath said, Come down!" (2Ki_1:9) Either they did not hold him to be a prophet, or they gloried in putting the power of their master above that of Jehovah. In any case, the insult was less against Elijah than Elijah's God.

There was no personal vindictiveness in the terrible reply of the old prophet. I don not suppose for a moment he considered the indignity done to himself. I believe he was filled with consuming zeal for the glory of God which had been trodden so rudely under foot and which he must vindicate in the eyes of Israel. "If I be a man of God, let fire come down from heaven and consume thee and thy fifty" (2Ki_1:12). And in a moment the fire leaped from its scabbard and laid the impious blasphemers low. That there was no malice in Elijah is clear from his willingness to go with the third captain, who spoke with reverence and humility. "And the angel of the LORD said unto Elijah, Go down with him: be not afraid of him. And he arose and went down with him unto the king" (2Ki_1:15).

A thought is suggested here of the meekness and gentleness of Christ. How wonderful it is to think that He who, by a single word, could have brought fire from heaven to destroy the bands that came to take Him in Gethsemane, left that word unspoken. He threw them on the ground for a moment, to show them how absolutely they were in His power, but He forbore to hurt one hair of their heads. It was a marvelous spectacle, which the legions of harnessed angels, who waited in midair for a word to bring them to His rescue, must have beheld with speechless amazement. The explanation is of course found in the fact that He was under the compulsion of a higher law -- the law of His Father's will, the law of self-sacrificing love, the law of a covenant sealed before the foundation of the world.

The only fire He sought was the fire of the Holy Ghost. "I am come to send fire on the earth; and what will I, if it be already kindled" (Luk_12:49). He strove not to avenge Himself or vindicate the majesty of His nature. Christ "endured the contradiction of sinners against himself" (Heb_12:3). "He is brought as a lamb to the slaughter, and as a sheep before his shearers is dumb, so he openeth not his mouth" (Isa_53:7). "When he was reviled, reviled not again; when he suffered, he threatened not; but committed himself to him that judgeth righteously" (1Pe_2:23). Oh, matchless meekness! Oh, wondrous self-control! Oh, glorious example of the spirit of His own teaching! May grace be given to each of us, His unworthy followers, to walk in His steps and to emulate His spirit, not calling for the fire of vengeance, but seeking the salvation of those who would do us hurt; dealing out not the fire of heaven, but those coals of fire which, heaped on the head of our adversaries, shall melt them into sweetness and gentleness and love.

There is also suggested here the impossibility of God ever condoning defiant and blasphemous sin. We have fallen on soft and degenerate days when, under false notions of charity and liberality, men are paring down their conceptions of the evil of sin and of the holy wrath of God, which is revealed from heaven against all ungodliness and unrighteousness of men.

It is quite true that God yearns over men with unutterable pleading tenderness. God is "not willing that any should perish, but that all should come to repentance" (2Pe_3:9). As there is not a dying sparrow in the recesses of the deepest woods over whose last agonies the Almighty does not bend with sympathetic interest and alleviating tenderness, so there is not one waif of humanity excluded from the warm zone of His infinite compassionateness and tender pity. In every outbreak of human sin, in the lot of every lost man and woman, over every street fight, at every public-house doorstep, amid the blasphemous orgies of every den of impurity and shame -- that love lingers, full of tears, and longings, and entreaties. "God so loved the world" (Joh_3:16).

And yet, side by side with this love of the sinner, there is God's hatred of his sin. This longsuffering lasts only so long as there is a possible hope of the transgressor turning from his evil ways. "If he turn not, He will whet His sword." The wrath of God against sinful men who have definitely elected their sin, slumbereth only; it is not dead. It broods over them, held back by His desire to give everyone the chance of salvation. They may be thankful, therefore, that their lot has fallen in this parenthesis of mercy. But "because sentence against their evil work is not executed speedily, therefore their hearts are fully set in them to do evil." Yet the time of forbearance will end at last, as the waiting did in the days of Noah. Then fire will fall, of which the material flame that fell on these insolent soldiers is a slight and imperfect symbol. And it shall be discovered how bitter a thing it is to encounter the wrath of the Lamb, "when the Lord Jesus shall be revealed from heaven with His mighty angels, in flaming fire taking vengeance on them that know not God, and that obey not the Gospel of our Lord Jesus Christ" (2Th_1:7-8).

We need more proclamation of this side of the Gospel. There is an alarming lack among us of the sense of sin. Our vast populations are indifferent to the message of mercy, because they have not been aroused with the message of the holy wrath of God against sin. We need again that one should come, in the power of Elijah, to do the work of John the Baptist; and to prepare men by the throes of conviction for the gentle ministry of Jesus Christ. The crying need of our times is a deeper conviction of sin. And if this shall be ever brought about, it must be by the religious teachers being led to study the Law as well as the Gospel, and to realize for themselves, as they can only do through the teaching of the Holy Spirit, the exceeding sinfulness of sin. Then when Elijah's fire of conviction has smitten human confidences low in the dust, there will be room for an Elisha to bind up broken hearts with the message of mercy.

We are also assured of Elijah's full restoration to the exercise of a glorious faith. In a former time, the message of Jezebel was enough to make him flee. But in this case he stood his ground, though an armed band came to capture him. It was as if he were able to repeat the familiar words without exaggeration: "Though an host should encamp against me, my heart shall not fear: though wars should rise against me, in this will I be confident" (Psa_27:3). And when he was bidden to go down with the third captain to the king, he did not hesitate; though it was to go through the streets of a crowded capital and into the very palace of his foes. We are reminded of the entrance of Luther into Worms, and of the remonstrance of Ambrose to the mightiest emperor of his time. Do you ask the secret of why he was able to stand so calmly beside the couch of the dying monarch, delivering his message and retiring unharmed? Ah, the answer is not far to seek. He was again dwelling in the secret of the Most High and standing in the presence of Jehovah. His faith was in lively and victorious exercise. He was able to gird himself with the panoply of God's mail, invulnerable to the darts of men and devils. And thus might he have spoken with himself as he passed through the threatening perils of that crisis: "By thee I have run through a troop: by my God have I leaped over a wall. As for God, his way is perfect... he is a buckler to all them that trust in him" (2Sa_22:30-31).

Is it not beautiful to behold this glorious out burst of the faith of Cherith, Zarephath, and Carmel? The old man, nearing his reward, was as vigorous in this as in his first challenge to Ahab. He bore fruit in old age, like one of God's evergreens which are full of sap. Glory be to Him who restores the soul of His faltering saints and brings them up from the grave and sets them again as stars in His right hand and deigns to use them once more in His glorious service!

Chapter Sixteen - Evensong

It was the cherished wish of Dr. Chalmers that he should be granted a Sabbatic decade, after the six decades of work, between the sixtieth and seventieth years of life, so completing its entire week. And it was surely a natural desire on the part of one who ranks among the foremost workers of our time. Whether or not this had been a specific desire of Elijah, in God's gracious providence it fell to his lot. And after a life full of storm and tempest, it came to pass that at eventide there was light and peace and a parenthesis of rest, as if the spirit of the world which he was about to enter were already shedding its spell over his path.

There is always something beautiful in the declining years of one who in earlier life has dared nobly and wrought successfully. Younger men gather around the veteran to whom they owe the inspiration and model of their lives, and call him father, enwreathing his gray locks with crowns in which love is entwined with reverence. Seeds sown years before and almost forgotten, or reckoned lost, yield their golden returns. Memory rescues from the oblivion of the past many priceless records, while hope, standing before the thinning veil, tells of things not perfectly seen as yet; but growing on the gaze of the ripened spirit. The old force still gleams in the eye, but its rays are tempered by that tenderness for human frailty and that deep self-knowledge which years alone can yield. The crudities are ripened, the harshnesses are softened, the bitternesses are mellowed. Marah waters no longer forbid the thirsty lips, but an Elim invites the weary. And from those revered lips flow rivers of wise and loving counsel to the younger generations grouped around. Such a life- evening seems to have been Elijah's. He did not reach a great old age. In all likelihood he showed no signs of physical decay. His eye was not dim nor his natural force abated. He probably betrayed his age more in the deeds he had done and in the mellowness of his spirit than in the infirmities of the natural man. Still there is little room for doubt that the noon of his life was well passed when he prepared himself for his final journey. And he must have been very grateful, as it was most fruitful of blessing to his country and to the cause of God, that there was granted a time of comparative calm at the close of his tempestuous career.

For those years of retirement were valuable in the highest degree, both in their immediate results upon hundreds of young lives, and in their far-off results on the coming times.

The Work of The Closing Years of Elijah's Life

His life has been called a one-man ministry, and there is much in it to warrant the description. He made his age. Towering above all the men of his time, he cleft his way through the crowds of meaner souls, and withstood the onslaughts of evil; as a rock shakes off the waves that break on it into volumes of spray. By heroic exploits and deeds of superhuman might, he strove single-handed against the tides of idolatry and sin that were sweeping over the land. In this he reminds us perpetually of Martin Luther and of John Knox; all these men were spiritual giants by reason of their faith, which could appropriate the power of God, as the lightning conductor can rob the thundercloud of its electric stores and bring them to the earth.

But though largely successful in keeping the cause of true religion from dying out, Elijah must often have realized the desirability of carrying on the work more systematically, and of leavening the country more thoroughly with the influence of devoted men. So, under Divine direction, he carefully fostered, if he did not altogether inaugurate, an institution which was a relic of former times, and known as the "schools of the prophets." When we use the word PROPHET, we think of it as indicating a person who can foretell the future, and much confusion is introduced into our reading of Scripture. It includes this idea as a fragment of a larger meaning. The original word means "boiling or bubbling over," and so a prophet was one whose heart was bubbling over with good matter, and with those Divine communications which struggled within him for utterance. He was a spiritual geyser, the mouthpiece and spokesman of God. "Holy men spake as they were moved by the Holy Ghost" (2Pe_1:21). So these schools of the prophets were colleges in which a number of young men gathered, their hearts open to receive, and their tongues to utter, the messages of God.

The Christian traveler among the Western Isles of Scotland will hardly fail to visit one small, bare, lone spot out amid the roll of the Atlantic waves. It is thy shore, Iona, of which I write! No natural beauties arrest the eye or enchain the interest. There is but one poor village with its two boats and squalid population. Yet who can visit that low shore and stand amid those crumbling ruins without intense emotions? It was there that Columba built the first Christian church to shed its gentle rays over those benighted regions and to shelter the young apostles who carried the Gospel throughout the pagan kingdoms of Northern Britain. With similar emotions should we stand amid the ruins of Bethel, Gilgal, and Jericho, where, in his declining years, Elijah gathered around him the flower of the seven thousand and educated them to receive and transmit something of his own spiritual force and fire. These were the missionary seminaries of the age, the repositories of sacred truth and learning; and beneath his influence, an Isaiah, a Hosea, an Ezekiel may have first received impulses which have since thrilled through the world.

These young men were formed into separate companies of fifty in different towns. They were called sons. The chief among them, like the abbot of a monastery, was called father. Clad in a simple dress, they had their food in common and dwelt in huts made of the branches of trees. They were well versed in the sacred books, which they probably transcribed for circulation, and read in the hearing of the people. They were frequently sent forth on errands of God's Spirit -- to anoint a king, to upbraid a high-handed sinner, or to take the part of oppressed and injured innocence. It was, therefore, no small work for Elijah to put these schools on so secure a basis that, when he was gone, they might perpetuate his influence and guard the flames which he had kindled.

The Attitude of His Spirit in Anticipating His Translation

The old man clung to those young hearts and felt that his last days could not be better spent than in seeing them once more; though he resolved to say nothing of his approaching departure or of the conspicuous honor that was shortly to be conferred on him. Here is the humility of true greatness! He foresaw that he was to enjoy an exodus to which, in the whole history of the race, there had been but one parallel. Yet he was so reticent about it that if he had had his way, no mortal eye would have beheld it. Anyone less great would have let the secret out, or have contrived to line the heights of the Jordan with expectant crowds of witnesses. Instead of this, he kept the secret well locked up within him and tried to dissuade Elisha from accompanying him a single step. "Tarry here" (2Ki_2:2). Perhaps that loyal heart feared attracting to himself, either then or afterward, honor due only to God.

Alas, what a rebuke is here for ourselves! The prophet's evident desire to die alone shames us when we remember how eager we are to tell men, by every available medium, of what we are doing for the Lord. There is not a talent with which He intrusts us which we do not parade as a matter of self-laudation. There is not a breath of success that does not mightily puff us up. What wonder that our Father dare not give us much marked success or many conspicuous spiritual endowments, lest we be tempted further to our ruin! Oh, when shall we be free of ourselves? Would that we could live so perpetually facing the sun that we might never see the dark shadow of self! "I could not see for the glory of that light." The Holy Spirit of life alone can set us free from the law of sin and death. Let us urge Him to hasten the performance of His gracious office and to give us the sweet humility of this man who was willing to efface himself that men might think only of his Master and Lord.

We are also deeply impressed by the calm tenor of the prophet's course through those closing days. He knew that before many suns had set he would be standing in the light of eternity, mingling with his peers, understanding all the mysteries that had puzzled his eager spirit, and beholding the face of God; and we might have expected him to fill the preceding hours with ecstatic offices of devotion. But instead, he spent the days, as he often spent them before, visiting the schools of the prophets and quietly conversing with his friend, until the chariot swept Elijah from his side. And, as we consider that spectacle, we learn that a good man should so live that he need make no extra preparation when death suddenly summons him, and that our best method of awaiting the great exchange of worlds is to go on doing the duties of daily life.

That was a wise and true reply of Wesley to the inquiry, "What would you do if you knew that you would have to die within three days?" "I should just do the work which I have already planned to do: ministering in one place; meeting my preachers in another; lodging in yet another, till the moment came that I was called to yield my spirit back to Him who gave it." When our summons comes, we should wish to be found, not in the place which sentiment or a false sense of religious propriety might suggest, but just doing the work which we have been appointed to do, and in the place where duty would demand our presence at that very hour. The workshop and the factory are as near heaven as the sanctuary; the God-given task as fair a height for ascension as Olivet or Pisgah.

The Affectionate Love with Which Elijah Was Regarded

It strongly showed itself in Elisha. The younger man stood with his revered leader, as for the last time he surveyed from the heights of Western Gilgal the scene of his former ministry. And, in spite of many persuasives to the contrary, he went with him down the steep descent to Bethel and Jericho. He followed him, even though they had to cross the Jordan, which meant death and judgment. The sacred historian accentuates the strength of their affection, as he says thrice over, they two went on; they two stood by the Jordan; they two went over. And again the strength of that love, which the cold waters of death could not extinguish, approved itself in the repeated asseveration: "As the LORD liveth, and as thy soul liveth, I will not leave thee" (2Ki_2:2). It is sweet to think that there were in the rugged, strong nature of Elijah such winsome qualities as could elicit so deep and tenacious an affection. We catch a glimpse of a tenderer side for which we had hardly given him credit.

Unusual emotion also welled up in the hearts of the young men, whose reverence shared the empire with their love, as they beheld their master for the last time. With delicate reticence they would not speak on a subject which he did not mention but, drawing Elisha aside, they asked him whether the moment of separation had not come. "Yes," said he in effect, "but do not speak of it. Let there be no parting scene. Give and receive the parting farewells in expressive silence."

But in all their intercourse, how real and near the Lord seemed! To Elijah it was the Lord who was sending him from place to place: "the

97

Lord hath sent me." To Elisha it was the living Lord to whom he constantly appealed: "as the Lord thy God liveth" -- living on the other side of the great change through which his master was to pass to Him. To the prophets, it was the Lord who was taking their head and leader to Himself. Surely those who speak thus have reached a position in which they can meet death without a tremor. And what is death but, as we shall see in our next chapter, a translation!

What is the Lord to you? Is He a dear and familiar friend, of whom you can speak with unwavering confidence? Then you need not fear to tread the verge of Jordan. Otherwise, it becomes you to get to His precious blood and to wash your garments white, that you may have right to the tree of life, and may enter in through the gates into the city.

Chapter Seventeen - The Translation

We have reached at length one of the most sublime scenes of Old Testament story. We should have been glad to learn the most minute particulars concerning it; but the historian contents himself with the simplest statements. Just one or two broad, strong outlines, and all is told that we may know. The veil of distance, or the elevation of the hills, was enough to hide the receding figures of the prophets from the eager gaze of the group that watched them from the neighborhood of Jericho. And the dazzling glory of the celestial cortege made the only spectator unable to scrutinize it too narrowly. What a wonder, then, if the narrative is given in one brief verse! "And it came to pass, as they still went on, and talked, that behold, there appeared a chariot of fire, and horses of fire, and parted them both asunder; and Elijah went up by a whirlwind into heaven" (2Ki_2:11).

But there was one symptom at least, of the coming wonder, which was clearly witnessed by more than the solitary companion who had so faithfully and tenaciously kept by Elijah's side. The two friends halted for a moment before the broad waters of the Jordan, which threatened to bar their onward steps, and then Elijah's spirit was thrilled with the old omnipotent faith such as had so often enabled him to overcome the working of natural laws, by the introduction of the laws of that higher sphere which only answer the summons of a mighty faith.

True, he took off his well-worn mantle and wrapped it together and smote the waters. But that, at the best, was only an outward and significant sign. At that same moment his spirit was grappling the power of the Infinite God and was bringing it to bear on the hurrying stream. He knew that the Lord had sent him thither, and that his road lay further into the country on the other side. He saw no means of pursuing the God-marked path. He was sure that, since his way led through the waters, God was prepared to make it possible and easy for him to tread it. And he therefore dared to strike the waters, believing that divine power was working in every stroke; and the waters parted hither and thither, leaving a clear passage, through which they went.

Child of God, your path seems sometimes to lie right through a flowing Jordan. There is no alternative but that you should go straight on. Forward moves the cloud. Forward points the signpost of circumstance. Forward bids the inward prompting. But how, when Jordan rolls in front? Now is the time for faith! Where God's finger points, there God's hand will make the way. Believe that it shall be so! Advance in unfaltering faith! Step down the shelving bank, and the waters of difficulty shall part before you; and you shall find a pathway where to human vision there was none. So through parting Jordans you shall march to your reward.

The Fitness of This Translation

There was fitness in the place, Not the smiling plain of Esdraelon, with its cornfields and vineyards and dotted hamlets, speaking of the toils and homes of men. Not the desert of Sinai, so closely allied with the memory of his fatal fall. Not the schools of Gilgal, Bethel, or Jericho. None of these would furnish a fit setting for his farewell to his earthly ministry. But, away from all these; amid the scenery familiar to his early life; in view of localities forever associated with the most memorable events of his nation's history; surrounded by the lonely grandeur of some rocky gorge -- there God chose to send His chariot to fetch him home.

There was fitness in the method. He had himself been as the whirlwind, that falls suddenly on the unsuspecting world, and sweeps all before it in its impetuous course, leaving devastation and ruin in its track. It was meet that a whirlwind-man should be swept to heaven in the very element of his life. His character was well depicted in the panorama of the desert, with its shivering wind and its glowing fire. And nothing could be more appropriate than that the stormy energy of his career should be set forth in the rush of the whirlwind; and the intensity of his spirit by the fire that flashed in the harnessed seraphim. What a contrast to the gently upward motion of the ascending Savior!

There was fitness in the exclamation with which Elisha bade him farewell. He cried, "My father, my father, the chariot of Israel, and the horsemen thereof" (2Ki_2:12). Doubtless, amid that sudden flash of glory he hardly knew what he said. Yet he closely hit the truth. That man, whom he had come to love as a father, had indeed been as an armed chariot of defense to Israel. By his faith and prayers and deeds, he had often warded off evil and danger with more certain success than could have been effected by an armed troop. Alas that such people are rare! But in our time we have known them; and when they have been suddenly swept from our side, we have felt as if the Church had been deprived of one main source of security and help.

The Reasons for This Translation

One of the chief reasons was, no doubt, **TO WITNESS TO HIS TIMES.**

The men of his day were plunged in sensuality and had little thought of the hereafter. At the very best, the Jews had but vague notions of the other life; and those notions were probably still further darkened by the obscuring influences of idolatry and sin. But here a convincing evidence was given that there was a spiritual world into which the righteous entered and that, when the body sank in death, the spirit did not share its fate but entered into a state of being in which its noblest instincts found their befitting environment and home -- fire to fire, spirit to spirit, the man of God to God.

A similar testimony was given to the men of his time by the rapture of Enoch before the Flood, and by the ascension of our Lord from the brow of Olivet. Where did these three wondrous journeys end, unless there was a bourn which was their befitting terminus and goal? And as the tidings spread, thrilling all listeners with mysterious awe, and as they heard that no sign of the rapt ones could be discovered by the most diligent search, would there not break upon them the conviction that they likewise would have to take that wondrous journey into the unseen, soaring beyond all worlds or sinking into the bottomless pit?

Another reason was evidently the desire on the part of God **TO GIVE A STRIKING SANCTION TO HIS SERVANT'S WORDS.**

How easy was it for the men of that time to evade the force of Elijah's ministry, by asserting that he was an enthusiast, an alarmist, a firebrand! It would be convenient for them to think that his denunciations and threats began and ended with himself -- the workings of a distempered brain. And if he had passed away in decrepit old age, they would have been still further encouraged in their impious conjecturings. How would they have known that he spoke the truth of God? But the mouths of blasphemers and gainsayers were stopped when God put such a conspicuous seal upon His servant's ministry. It was as if Jehovah had stepped out of the unseen to vindicate him and to affirm that he was His chosen ambassador, and that the word in his lips was true. The translation was to the lifework of Elijah what the resurrection was to that of Jesus -- it was God's irrefragable testimony to the world.

As a servant, Elijah had failed in one fatal moment; and by that moment's failure had missed a splendid chance: but for all that, the general tenor of his ministry was such as God could approve; and concerning it He could bear His sanctioning testimony to men. It may sometimes happen that our Father will greatly honor His servants in the eyes of men, while He will be very strict in His private dealings with them in reference to certain failures in duty of which only He and they are aware.

The Lessons of This Translation for Ourselves

LET US TAKE CARE NOT TO DICTATE TO GOD.

This was the man who lay down upon the ground and asked to die. If he had had his will, he would have had the desert sands for his shroud and the desert winds for his requiem. How good it was of God to refuse him the answer he craved! Was it not better to pass away, missed and beloved, in the chariot which his Father had sent for him, and with which Ahab's, though he had run before it, could bear no comparison?

This is no doubt one reason why our prayers go unanswered. We know not what we ask. We ask for things which we would not dream of, if we only knew the infinite superiority of the lot which our Father has planned out for us. We shall have to bless Him forever, more for the prayers He refused than for those He granted. When next your request is denied, reflect that it may be because God is preparing something for you as much better than your request as the translation of Elijah was better than his own petition for himself.

LET US LEARN WHAT DEATH IS.

It is simply a transfer: not a state, but an act; not a condition, but a passage. We pass through a doorway, we cross a bridge of smiles, we flash from the dark into the light. There is no interval of unconsciousness, no parenthesis of suspended animation. "Absent from the body," we are instantly "present with the Lord" (2Co_5:8). Oh, do not think of death as the jailer of a prison in which he is collecting the saints against some final order for their liberty. It is nothing of the sort. It is but the grim disguise of one of the angels of God's presence-chamber, specially commissioned to bring faithful souls into the audience-room of the King. As by the single act of birth we entered into this lower life, so by the single act -- which men call death, but which the angels call birth (for Christ is the Firstborn from among the dead) -- we pass into the real life. The fact that Elijah appeared on the transfiguration mount in holy converse with Moses and Christ proves that the blessed dead are really the living ones; sentient, active, intensely in earnest; and they entered that life in a single moment, the moment of death. Would it not be truer to speak of them not as the dead, but as those who have died and are alive forever? It must be remembered, however, that while it is far better for the emancipated soul and spirit to be with Christ, present with the Lord, the blessedness will not be complete until the resurrection of the body, which will then have put on incorruption and immortality.

LET US SEE HERE A TYPE OF THE RAPTURE OF THE SAINTS.

We do not know what change passed over the mortal body of the ascending prophet. This is all we know, that "mortality is swallowed up of life" (2Co_5:4). There was wrought on him a change like that which took place in the grave of Joseph, when the crucified body of Jesus became transformed into the risen body -- which was largely independent of the laws of nature, but which was so like the body which He had worn for thirty-three years that it was readily and universally recognized. Corruption put on incorruption. The mortal put on immortality. The body of humiliation was exchanged for the body of glory.

Such a change, unless Christ tarry longer than the term of our natural life, shall be the portion of many who read these lines -- "caught up... to meet the Lord in the air" (1Th_4:17). It becomes us then to walk as Elijah did, with alert and watchful spirit; talking only on themes that would not be inconsistent with an instantaneous flash into the presence of God. Thus, whenever our Father's carriage comes for us, and wherever it overtakes us -- whether in the storm at sea, or in the railway accident; in the tumult of a catastrophe, or in the gradual decay of prolonged illness -- may we be prepared to step in, and sweep through the gates, washed in the blood of the Lamb!

Was it not some reference to this august event that was in the mind of the great Welsh preacher, Christmas Evans, who, when dying, majestically waved his hand to the bystanders and looked upward with a smile and uttered these last words, "Drive on!" "The chariots of God are twenty thousand" (Psa_68:17). May we not suppose that one awaits each departing spirit, standing ready at hand to convey it into the presence of the King, to whom be glory for ever and ever!

Chapter Eighteen - A Double Portion of Elijah's Spirit

There is one incident forever associated with the translation of Elijah, which, though it largely concerns his friend and successor, is so characteristic of the great prophet himself that we must not pass it over without some notice. It is deeply significant. We are told that, after they had passed the Jordan, the two friends went on and talked. What sublime themes must have engaged them, standing as they did on the very confines of heaven and in the vestibule of eternity. Israel's apostasy and approaching doom; the ministry just closing, with its solemn warnings; the outlook toward the work upon which Elisha was preparing to enter -- these and cognate subjects must have occupied them.

It was in the course of this conversation that "Elijah said unto Elisha, Ask what I shall do for thee, before I be taken away from thee" (2Ki_2:9). It was a very wide door flung open by the elder to his younger friend. And at first we are surprised to think that Elijah could offer to supply anything for which Elisha asked. Is not this rather the prerogative of God? Surely God alone can do whatsoever we desire when we pray, and even He is limited by the fulfillment, on our part, of certain essential conditions. But we must remember that Elijah was intimately familiar with the mind and heart of his brother. It was not in vain that they had spent those years of ministry together. It was with the object of testing the spirit of his friend that the departing prophet had urged him again and again to leave him. And it was only when Elisha had stood the test with such unwavering resolution that Elijah was able to give him this carte blanche . He knew that Elisha would ask nothing for which he could not exercise his mighty faith, or which God could not and would not bestow. He was only a man of like passions with ourselves, cast in the ordinary mold of human nature but, by close and intimate communion with God, he had reached such a pitch of holy boldness that the very keys of spiritual blessing seemed put into his hand so that he might dispense to kindred spirits the priceless gifts of God. Why should not we strive after and attain similar precious faith?

Elisha's Large Request

Elijah's confidence was not misplaced. Elisha's reply wrought along those lines which he had anticipated. He sought neither wealth, nor position, nor worldly power, nor a share in those advantages on which he had turned his back forever when he said farewell to home and friends and worldly prospects. "And Elisha said, I pray thee, let a double portion of thy spirit be upon me" (2Ki_2:9).

What did Elisha mean by this request? I do not interpret his request to mean that he should have twice as much of the faith and spiritual force as characterized his master. What he intended was to ask that he might be considered as Elijah's eldest son, the heir to his spirit, the successor to his work. There is a passage in the law of Moses which clearly proves that "the double portion" was the right of the firstborn and heir (Deu_21:17). This the prophet sought, and this he certainly obtained.

It was a noble request. He was evidently called to succeed to Elijah's work, but he felt that he dare not undertake its responsibilities, or face its inevitable perils, unless he were specially equipped with spiritual power. It is not often that we can count an Elijah among our friends, but when we may, we shall do well to invoke his intercessions on our behalf that we may be endowed with a similar spirit. And there is at least One to whom we can all go with this sublime request, sure that He is more eager to give us His Holy Spirit than the tenderest earthly father to satisfy his children's hunger with bread. Oh, for this spiritual hunger, insatiable for the best gifts! Men of the world hunger for name and rank and wealth, and they get what they seek because they will take no nay. Blessed should we be if we were as eager after the Spirit of God; and if, instead of giving up opportunities of usefulness because we did not feel qualified to fill them, we rather sought and received a new baptism of power, a fresh endowment of the Holy Spirit.

Who need shrink from attempting Elijah's work if first we have received Elijah's spirit? Instead of relinquishing a work for which you do not feel naturally qualified, wait in the fervency of entreaty and in the expectancy of faith, until you are endued with power from on high. There is no work to which God calls you for which He is not prepared to qualify you. Let it never be forgotten that Elijah himself did what he did, not by inherent qualities, but because through faith he had received such copious bestowments of the Spirit of God; and what he did we may do again -- the weakest and humblest of us -- if only we are prepared to wait and watch and pray until our Pentecost breaks upon us, with or without its sound of rushing wind and its tongues of flaming fire.

Let Us Clearly Understand the Two Conditions Imposed on Elisha

1. TENACITY OF PURPOSE.

Elijah tested it severely at every step of that farewell journey. Repeatedly he said, "Tarry here" (2Ki_2:2). But He might as well have tried to uproot a cedar of Lebanon or stir Carmel from its base. Neither Gilgal with its panoramic scenery, nor Bethel with its memories of the angel-haunted dream, nor Jericho, the border town, were able to attract or retain him. And though their course lay through the Jordan flood of death, it sufficed not to deter that eager spirit. Elisha knew what he sought; he read the meaning of the discipline to which he was being exposed, and his heroic resolution grew with the ordeal, as the waters of a stream grow against an arresting dam until they overleap it and rush merrily on their way. It was thus that the Syro-Phoenician woman prevailed with Christ. It was thus that the apostles waited for the promise of the Father, undaunted by ten days' delay.

Before giving us the Holy Ghost, our Father will certainly try us to see if we can live without Him. If we can, we may. And it is only when we give signs of a resolution which will take no denial, but detains the Angel with its imperative importunity and vows its unalterable determination to be blessed -- it is only then that God who had never been really reluctant and had only been testing us, turns to us with a smile and says, "O child, great is thy importunity; be it unto thee even as thou wilt." "The kingdom of heaven suffereth violence, and the violent take it by force" (Mat_11:12).

How often we persuade ourselves that we can acquire the greatest spiritual blessings without paying the equivalent price! Thus James and John thought that they could obtain a seat each on the throne for the asking. They did not realize that the cross preceded the crown, and that the bitter cup of Gethsemane lay between them and the coronation anthem. We must pass through the Jordan; daily must we take up the cross and follow Jesus; we must be conformed to Him in the likeness of His death and in the fellowship of His sufferings; the old nature must be crucified; the divine will must be lovingly accepted, though it cost tears of blood and bitter sorrow. Then, having evinced the steadfastness of our purpose, we shall approve ourselves worthy to be the recipients of God's supreme gift.

SPIRITUAL INSIGHT.

"If thou see me when I am taken from thee, it shall be so unto thee; but if not, it shall not be so" (2Ki_2:10). There was nothing arbitrary in this demand. And it would have been hardly possible to have devised a more complete criterion of the spiritual condition of this eager aspirant. To see the transactions of the spirit world requires a spirit of no ordinary purity and of no ordinary faith. No mere mortal eye could have beheld that fiery cortege. To senses dulled with passion or blinded by materialism, the space occupied by the flaming seraphim would have seemed devoid of any special interest, and bare as the rest of the surrounding scenery. Perhaps there was not another individual in all Israel with heart pure enough, or spiritual nature keen enough, to have been sensible of that glorious visitation. Had we been there, we should probably have been unconscious of anything, save the sudden disappearance of the prophet. But since Elisha saw it all, it is clear that his passions were under control; his temper refined; his spiritual life in healthy exercise; and his whole being of such an order as to admit him into the foremost rank of the spiritual world without risk. Such must we be, by the grace of God, before we can aspire to possess or wield similar powers. Our reception of the Spirit will be in exact proportion to the subjection of the flesh, and the consequent vigor of our inner life.

The Answer

"He took up also the mantle of Elijah that fell from him." Ah, that falling mantle! How much it meant! It is said that the bestowal of the mantle has always been considered by Eastern people an indispensable part of consecration to a sacred office. When, therefore, Elijah's mantle fluttered to Elisha's feet, he knew at once that heaven itself had ratified his request. He knew that he had Elijah's post. He believed that he was anointed with Elijah's power. I do not for a moment think that there was any emotional or sensible indication of the mighty change which had been wrought upon him. His spirit was still. There was no tremor in his pulse; no thrill of consciously added power in his frame. The torrent of spiritual force had entered him as quietly as light enters the world, and as the forces of spring thrill through the woods.

If, in patience and faith, we claim of our Father the filling of the Holy Ghost, we must never ask ourselves if we feel full. We must believe that God has kept His word with us, and that we are filled, though no celestial sign accompanies the entering glory of that power "which works effectually in them that believe." But others will become aware of the presence of something that we never had before as they see us stand by some tameless Jordan and behold the turbulent waters part hither and thither before our stroke.

Directly we receive some great spiritual endowment, we may expect to have it tested. It was so with Elisha. He "went back, and stood by the bank of the Jordan" (2Ki_2:13). Did he hesitate? If so, it was but for a moment. He had seen Elijah go; and he believed, though probably he did not feel, that therefore the double portion of his spirit had fallen to his lot. He therefore acted upon the assurance of his faith. "He took the mantle of Elijah that fell from him, and smote the waters, and said, Where is the LORD God of Elijah? and when he also had smitten the waters, they parted hither and thither: and Elisha went over. And when the sons of the prophets which were to view at Jericho saw him, they said, The spirit of Elijah doth rest on Elisha" (2Ki_12:14-15).

As soon as Jesus had been anointed with the Holy Ghost, He was led into the wilderness to be tempted. The title "Son of God," uttered over the waters of baptism, was made the subject of Satan's wildest attacks: "If Thou be the Son of God,..." So must it be ever. But difficulty, temptation, and trial, avail to bring into greater prominence, both for ourselves and others, the reality and glory of the blessing we have received. The parted Jordan proves the presence of the Spirit.

"Where is the Lord God of Elijah?" That cry has often been raised when the Church, bereft of its leaders, has stood face to face with some great and apparently insuperable difficulty. And sometimes there has been more of despair than hope in the cry. But though Elijah goes, Elijah's God remains. He takes His weary workers home, but He is careful to supply their place and to anoint others to carry on their work. It is His work, not ours. On Him is the responsibility, as to Him shall be the glory. If you ask where He is, an answer close behind you whispers, "I am here." Catch up the mantle of the departed. Emulate their lives. Seek their spirit. Smite the bitter waves of difficulty in unwavering faith, and you shall find that the Lord God of Elijah will do as much for you as for the saints who have been swept to their reward and are now mingling with the great cloud of witnesses that are watching your conflicts, your triumphs, and your joys.

Chapter Nineteen - The Transfiguration

Wordsworth and all his followers were students in the school of Jesus Christ. Never breathed a more enthusiastic lover of nature than He. Lilies could not grow at His feet, or birds wing their homeward flight over His head, without attracting His swift attention. His daily talk was of wandering sheep and whitening corn, of living wells and summer rain, of the changing hues of morn and eve. We cannot wonder, therefore, at His snatching brief opportunities for communion with the scenes of natural beauty, or that He often climbed the everlasting hills -- the natural altars of the world -- obviously intended not for habitation, but for worship.

Such an occasion is the one referred to here. Wearied with His toils and requiring time for private intercourse with His friends to prepare them for the approaching tragedy, of which they were strangely unconscious, He traveled northward with His disciples, avoiding the larger towns, until they reached one of the smaller villages nestling on the lower slopes of Mount Hermon, which towers into the clouds and forms a majestic barrier on the northern frontier of Palestine. There they seem to have rested for about a week. Think how they may have spent those days! Watching the snows on the upper peaks flush in the dawn and glow in the sunset, as if aflame. Reveling in the fertility, which centuries before had been compared to the fragrant oil anointing the high priest. Visiting the ancient forest of cedars from which Hiram's servants had hewn the beams of Solomon's temple; or the mountain springs, where the familiar Jordan had its source. A week would quickly pass amid engagements such as these, blended, as they must have been, with intercourse on the loftiest themes.

After eight days, Jesus took with Him His three mighties -- Peter, James, and John; and as the evening shadows darkened over the world, He led them up to some neighboring summit, removed from the sight and sound of men. He went to brace Himself for the coming conflict by prayer, and perhaps for the earlier part of the night the favored three bore Him fellowship. But they soon grew weary, and presently, as afterward in Gethsemane, were wrapt in heavy sleep -- though dimly conscious of their Master's presence as He poured out His soul with strong cryings and tears. We know not how many hours elapsed before they were suddenly startled from their slumbers -- not by the gentle touch of morning light, but beneath the stroke of the unbearable glory which streamed from their Master's person, The fashion of His countenance was altered; the deep lines of care that had seamed it were obliterated; the look of pensive sadness was gone. "His face did shine as the sun;" not lit up as that of Moses was, by reflection from without, but illumined from within, as if the hidden glory of the Shekinah, too long concealed, were bursting through the veil of flesh, kindling it to radiance as it passed. "His raiment" -- the common homespun of the country -- "was white and glistering;" more resplendent than the glistening snow above, as though angels had woven it of light. But perhaps the greatest marvel of all was the presence of the august pair "which were Moses and Elias: who appeared in glory and spake of his decease [His exodus -- out of death into new and resurrection life] which he should accomplish at Jerusalem" (Luk_9:30-31).

Consider the Probable Reasons Why These Two, and Especially Elijah, were Chosen on This Sublime Occasion

THE FIRST REASON MIGHT HAVE BEEN THAT THEY COULD ATTEST THE DIGNITY OF THE LORD JESUS.

He was approaching the darkest hour of His career when His sun should set in an ocean of ignominy and shame, and it seemed as if heaven itself were astir, by delegation, to assure His friends and convince the world of His intrinsic worth. Should seraphs be commissioned? Nay; for men, unable to realize their rank, would be simply dazzled. Better far to send back someone of the human family who had passed into the unseen, but whose illustrious deeds still lived in the memory of mankind, giving weight to his witness. Yet who should be selected?

There might have been a fitness in sending the first Adam to attest the supreme dignity of the second, or Abraham, the father of them that believe. But their claims were waived in favor of these two who might have more weight with the men of that time, as representing the two great departments of Jewish thought and Scripture: Moses, the founder of the Law; Elijah, the greatest of the prophets.

It is impossible to exaggerate the prominence given to Elijah in the Jewish mind. At the circumcision of a child, a seat was always placed for Elijah; and at the annual celebration of the Passover in each home, wine was placed for him to drink -- the cup for which richer Jews, was made of gold and set with jewels. And it was universally believed that Elijah was to come again to announce the advent of the Messiah. It would, therefore, have great weight with these disciples, and through them with after ages, to feel that he had stood beside Jesus of Nazareth, offering Him homage and help. And it was partly the memory of the allegiance rendered by Elijah to his Master that led Peter to say, in after years, that he had been an eyewitness of His majesty.

Astronomers tell us that our sun, with its attendant worlds, is only a satellite of some other mightier star; and that these wondrous orbs are circling around some distant center, known as Alcyone. If this is so, and if our mighty sun is only a satellite, what must not be the glories of the central body, whose majestic progress it attends! And if Elijah were so illustrious, what must not be the glories of that wondrous Being to whom he was only a servant among many!

ANOTHER REASON MAY BE FOUND IN THE PECULIAR CIRCUMSTANCES UNDER WHICH THEY LEFT THE WORLD.

Moses died, not by disease or by natural decay, but beneath the kiss of God. His spirit passed painlessly and mysteriously to glory, while God buried his body. Elijah did not die. Disease and old age had nothing to do in taking down the fabric of his being. He did not sleep; but he was "changed in a moment, in the twinkling of an eye." We may not penetrate into the secrets of that mysterious borderland, which these two passed and repassed, in their holy ministry to the Savior's spirit; but we feel that there was something in the method of their departure from our world, which made that passage easier.

YET ANOTHER REASON IS SUGGESTED IN THE EVIDENT FULFILLMENT OF THEIR MINISTRY.

They had been originally sent to prepare for Christ. "We have found him," said Philip, "of whom Moses in the law and the prophets did write" (Joh_1:45). "For he [Moses]," Jesus said, "wrote of me" (Joh_5:46). "The testimony of Jesus is the spirit of prophecy" (Rev_19:1-21; Rev_10:1-11). But the Jews were in danger of forgetting this, and of attaching more importance to the messengers than was justifiable. They clung to the stars even when the sun was steadily climbing up the sky. It was the death warrant of Stephen that he seemed to them to slight the Old Testament by hinting that it would be abrogated and superseded by the New. Peter himself was quite prepared to treat Moses and Elijah on an equality with his Master by building three tabernacles -- one for each. This could not be, and therefore Moses and Elijah were swept away by a cloud, and Jesus only was left, and the voice of God was heard insisting that Peter and the two other disciples should listen to Him alone. It was as though God had said -- uttering words that lifted a dispensation from its hinges -- "As ye have listened to the Law and the Prophets, so now listen to My Son. Do not put yourselves again under the law, or rest content with the prophets, however lofty their ideals and burning their words; but give to Him all the veneration and attention that you have been hitherto wont to reserve for them. Pass from the anticipation to the reality; from the type to the perfect fulfillment. They are taken; but all that made them helpful is left."

We too must sometimes climb transfiguration mounts and see our beloved caught away from our gaze, and then return toward an unkindly and wrangling world. But let us remember that our hearts are bereft of their supports to drive us to find all, and more than all, in Jesus. He is enough for any heart, however lonely and desolate. He suffices for heaven, and surely He can for earth. All that is good in anyone was first in Him, and remains in Him forever without alloy. And as one after another is caught away, we are still rich with unsearchable wealth; we are still able to cope with all the devils that await us in the vales beneath, though we have "no man, save Jesus only" (Mat_17:8).

Such may have been some of the reasons that led to the appearance of these two men on the transfiguration mount: standing there for a moment and then receding into the land of glory from which they came; attesting His dignity and then withdrawing -- that the interest excited by their presence might not be focused on themselves, but turned at once and more intensely on the person of Jesus Christ.

Consider the Theme on Which They Spoke

They spoke not of the latest tidings of heaven; nor of their own wondrous past; nor of the distant future: but of the decease (lit. THE EXODUS) which He was to accomplish so soon at Jerusalem.

Great men love great thoughts. And where could there have been found greater subjects than this wondrous death and His glorious resurrection, which were to affect all worlds, and to involve the Son of God in shame and sorrow so unfathomable! Herein Moses and Elijah precede the greatest thinkers of mankind -- Galileo, Kepler, Newton, Milton, Faraday, who have sought in the Gospel of the cross the sea-room needed by their leviathan intellects.

Heaven was full of this theme. Angels, forsaking all other interests, were absorbed in wonder, awe, and love, as they watched each step toward the destined goal. May we not imagine all the life of heaven arrested and pausing before that stupendous tragedy? It was natural, then, that these latest comers from those shores should talk of the one all-engrossing topic in the land which they had left.

Their own salvation depended on the issue of that wondrous death. If ever there were men who might have stood a chance of being accepted on their own merits, surely these were such. But they would have been most particular in disclaiming any such distinction. Looking back on their careers, they were deeply sensible of their imperfections and their sins. Moses remembered the petulance of Massah. Elijah recalled the faithlessness and fretfulness of the desert. And, in the light of eternity, they saw evil in many things which had seemed passably good in the twilight of earth. They had no merits of their own. Their only hope of salvation lay where ours does -- in His overcoming the sharpness of death and opening the kingdom of heaven to all believers.

And surely our Lord would lead them to dwell on a theme so constantly present to His mind. He had always anticipated the hour of His death. It was for this that He had been born. But now it seemed very near. He stood within the shadow of the cross. And it must have been grateful to Him to talk with these lofty spirits of the various aspects of the joy that was set before Him. Moses might remind Him that if, as God's Lamb, He must die, yet as God's Lamb He would redeem countless myriads. Elijah might dwell on the glory that would accrue to the Father. These thoughts were familiar enough to the mind of our blessed Master; yet they must have gladdened and strengthened Him, as they fell from other lips. The more so, when they conversed together on the certain splendor of the resurrection morning that should follow His decease.

Let us learn how men view the work of Christ in the light of eternity. They do not dwell primarily on the mystery of the holy incarnation, or on the philanthropy of His life, or on the insight of His teachings. All these things are dwarfed by comparison with His death. That is His masterpiece -- the Mont Blanc of the glorious range of His achievements in our mortal flesh. Here the attributes of God find their most complete and most harmonious exemplification. Here the problems of human sin and salvation are met and solved. Here the travail of creation meets with its answer and key. Here are sown the seeds of the new heavens and earth in which shall dwell righteousness and peace. Here is the point of unity between all ages, all dispensations, all beings, all worlds. Here blend men and angels, departed spirits and the denizens of other spheres, Peter, James, and John, with Moses and Elijah; and all with the great God Himself, whose voice is heard falling in benediction from the opened heaven.

The nearer we get to the cross and the more we meditate on the decease accomplished at Jerusalem, the closer we shall come into the center of things, the deeper will be our harmony with ourselves and all other noble spirits and God Himself. Climb that mountain often, in holy reverie, and remember that in all the universe there is no spirit more deeply interested in the mysteries and meaning of our Savior's death than that noble prophet who now seeks no higher honor than to stand forever as near to the beloved Master as he did for one brief space on the transfiguration mount.

Chapter Twenty - "Filled with the Holy Spirit"

What may not one man do in one brief life, if he is willing to be simply a living conduit-pipe through which the power of God may descend to men? There is no limit to the possible usefulness of such a life. There is, on the one hand, the oceanic fullness of God; on the other, the awful need and desolation of man; guilty, weak, bankrupt, diseased: all that is required is a channel of communication between the two. When that channel is made and opened and kept free from the silting sand, there will ensue one great, plenteous, and equable flow of power carrying the fullness of God to the weary emptiness of man.

There is a splendid illustration in the life of Elijah, of which we are now taking our farewell. For more than a hundred years the tide had been running strongly against the truth of God. Idolatry had passed from the worship of Jereboam's calves to that of Baal and Astarte, with the licentious orgies and hideous rites which gathered around the ancient worship of the forces of nature. The system was maintained by an immense organization of wily priests who had settled down upon the national life like a fungus growth, striking its roots into the heart. The court was in its favor. The throne was occupied by a decadent man, the weak tool of his unscrupulous and beautiful wife -- the Lady Macbeth of Jewish history. Jehovah's altars were thrown down, His prophets silenced and in hiding, His faithful worshipers a mere handful whose existence was so secret as to be known only to Him. The lamp of truth had been overturned, and there was only a tiny spark of light feebly burning to show where once the light of true religion brightly shone.

Into such a state of things Elijah came, unarmed, from his native transJordanic hills; a highlander, unkempt, unpolished, unaccustomed to the manners of a court or the learning of the schools. Withal, a man weak where we are weak, tempted where we are tempted, of like passions with ourselves. And at once the tide began to turn. The progress of idolatry received a decisive check. The existence and power of Jehovah were vindicated. New courage was infused into the timid remnant of truehearted disciples. Altars were rebuilt, colleges were opened for the training of the godly youth, a successor was appointed, and an impetus given to the cause of truth, which was felt for many generations.

Perhaps the greatest tribute to Elijah's power with his contemporaries is in the fact that his name and work stood out in bold and clear outline for nine hundred years after his death, surpassing the whole school of Jewish prophets, as the Jungfrau rears her snowclad peaks above the giants of her chain; and furnishing a model with which to set forth the power and courage of the forerunner of our Lord. The Holy Spirit, speaking in Malachi, the last of the prophets, could find no better symbol of John the Baptist than to compare him with the famous prophet who, centuries before, had swept to heaven in the chariot of flame: "Behold, I will send you Elijah the prophet before the great and dreadful day of the LORD" (Mal_4:5). The bright angel Gabriel, standing, four hundred years after, amid the ascending incense of the holy place, found no easier method of conveying to the aged priest the type of the wondrous son that was to gladden his old age, than to liken him to Elijah: "He shall go before him in the spirit and power of Elias" (Luk_1:17).

Whenever a notable religious movement was stirring through the land, the people were accustomed to think that the prophet of Carmel had again returned to earth; and thus the deputation asked John the Baptist, saying, "Art thou Elijah?" and when a mightier than John had set all men musing in their hearts, as the disciples told our Lord, many of the common people believed that the long expectation of centuries was realized, and that Elijah was risen again. It was commonly believed that no other born of a woman was great enough to precede the Messiah, and that he would anticipate His advent by an interval of three days, during which he should proclaim, in a voice heard over all the earth, peace, happiness, and salvation.

All these things are evidences of the towering greatness of Elijah's character and work. With all the failures and mistakes to which such natures are prone, he was a great man and did a noble work. And the secret of all was to be found not in any intrinsic qualities, but in the fact that he was filled with the Holy Ghost. Let us pause here and ask ourselves if we can give our thoughtful assent to this statement. If we cannot, we must count much of our time and labor in these chapters wasted, for our one aim has been to establish this point. But if we can, then, as we close these chapters of stirring sacred biography, we may resolve that we will never rest until we too are filled with the Holy Ghost. We will not rest satisfied in being imitators merely, but we will seek to be filled with the same Spirit, that He may work again through us the marvels of the past.

If I may venture so to put it, God is in extremity for men who, thoughtless for themselves, will desire only to be receivers and channels of His power. He will take young men and women, old men and children, servants and handmaidens in the waning days of this era and will fill them with the selfsame Spirit whose power was once reserved for a favored few. Besides all this, the positive command has never been repealed which bids us be "filled with the Spirit" (Eph_5:18). And we cannot reiterate too often that those who feel themselves bound to strict temperance in respect to wine by the former clause, should feel the latter one to be equally imperative. Moreover, what God commands, He is prepared to do all that is needful on His side to effect. Then when, like John the Baptist, we are filled with the Holy Ghost, like John the Baptist we "shall go before him in the spirit and power of Elias, to turn the hearts of the fathers to the children, and the disobedient to the wisdom of the just; to make ready a people prepared for the Lord" (Luk_1:17).

This Filling of the Holy Ghost Was the Characteristic of the Church

On the day of Pentecost they were all filled with the Holy Ghost -- women as well as men, obscure disciples as well as illustrious apostles -- and, to guard against the leakage which is, alas, too common to us all, they were filled and filled again. Those who are described as filled in Act_2:4 are spoken of as filled again in Act_4:31. New converts, like Saul of Tarsus, were bidden to expect this blessed filling. Deacons called to do the secular business of the Church must be men filled with the Holy Ghost. That he was a good man, full of the Holy Ghost, was a greater recommendation of Barnabas than that he had parted with his lands. And even churches, like those in the highlands of Galatia, were no sooner brought in to existence by the labors of the apostle Paul than they were filled with the Holy Ghost. In point of fact, the Christians of the first age were taught to expect this blessed filling. And the early Church was a collection of Spirit-filled people. Probably it was the exception, rather than the rule, not to be filled with the blessed presence of God and the Holy Ghost.

There is no formal conclusion to the book of Acts, because God meant the story to be prolonged through the ages, after the same manner. Let us not think that God resembles some, who put a portico of marble to a building which they finish with common brick. He did not give an experience at Pentecost which He either would not or could not maintain. Pentecost was simply meant to be the specimen and type of all the days of all the years of the present age. And if our times seem to have fallen far below this blessed level, it is not because of any failure on God's part, but because the Church has neglected this holy doctrine. Christians have seemed to suppose that the filling of the Holy Ghost was the prerogative of a few. The majority of them have never thought of it as within their reach, and the Church has been simply paralyzed for want of the only power that can avail her in her conflict against the world -- a power which was distinctly pledged to her by her ascending Lord. We never can regain or hold our true position until all believers see that the filling of the Holy Ghost is equally for them as for the first Christians, and that the barriers are broken down which once limited it to a few. We do not seek the sound of rushing wind, or the coronet of flame, or the special gifts which were conferred for a special purpose: these are the minor accessories of this filling, with which we can dispense. But what we cannot dispense with and must not dream of missing is the distinct filling of the Holy Ghost. No doubt He is in us if we are Christians, but we must never be content until He is in us in power -- not a breath, but a mighty wind; not a rill, but a torrent; not an influence, but a mighty, energizing Person.

We Must Comply with Certain Conditions If We Would Be Filled

WE MUST DESIRE TO BE FILLED FOR THE GLORY OF GOD.

A lady told me lately that she had long been seeking the power of the Spirit, but in vain. She could not understand the cause of her failure, until she came to see that she was seeking Him for the joy that He would bring rather than for the glory that would accrue to God. Ah, we must seek for the Spirit's power, not for our happiness or comfort, nor yet for the good that we may be the better able to effect; but that Christ may be magnified in our bodies, whether by life or death.

WE MUST BRING CLEANSED VESSELS.

God will not deposit His most precious gift in unclean receptacles. And we need cleansing in the precious blood before we can presume to expect that God will give us what we seek. We cannot expect to be free from indwelling sin, but we may at least be washed in the blood of Christ from all conscious filthiness and stain.

WE MUST BE PREPARED TO LET THE HOLY SPIRIT DO AS HE WILL WITH US AND THROUGH US.

There must be no reserve, no holding back, no contrariety of purpose. The whole nature must be unbarred, and every part yielded. There is a law in physics that forces work in the direction of least resistance. Let us present no resistance whatever to the working of the Holy Ghost. He who resists least will possess most. God gives the Holy Ghost to them that obey Him (Act_5:32).

WE MUST APPROPRIATE HIM BY BIRTH.

There is no need for us to wait ten days, because the Holy Spirit has been given to the church. This is included in the spiritual blessings with which our Father has blessed us in Christ Jesus. We need not struggle and agonize and convulse ourselves in the vehemence of entreaty; we have simply to take what God has allotted to us and is waiting to impart. Open your mouth wide, and He will fill it. Dig the ditches, and though you can discern no evidences of the entering floods, they shall be filled. Ask as a little child asks for its breakfast already on the table. So soon as you ask, you do receive. Though you experience no rush of transcendent joy, go your way reckoning yourself filled, whether you feel so or not. As the days go on, you will find that you have been filled, and are being filled, with new power and joy and wealth. You will not long be left to the reckoning of faith, for you will be made aware of a virtue going out from you, which shall heal and save.

Time Would Fail to Enumerate All the Blessings That Will Ensue

The presence of the Holy Ghost in the heart, in all His glorious fullness, cannot be hid. It will surely betray itself as the presence of the everburning fire in the hothouse is indicated by the luxuriance of flower and fruit within its tropical inclosure, while frost and snow reign in the world without. There will be no effort, no striving after great effect, no ostentatious show. He distills as the dew upon the tender herb and descends as the summer showers upon the mown grass. This conception of His work is clearly taught by the word selected by the apostle to describe the results of His indwelling. He speaks of them as the "fruit of the Spirit," in contrast to the "works of the flesh" (Gal_5:16-26); and what deep suggestions of quiet growth, and exquisite beauty, and spontaneousness of life lie in that significant phrase!

In passing, we can do no more than enumerate some of the results of the indwelling of the Holy Ghost.

THERE IS VICTORY OVER SIN.

The law of the Spirit of life in Christ Jesus makes us free from the law of sin and death, just as the law of the elasticity of the air makes the bird free from the predominating power of the pull of gravitation.

THERE IS THE INDWELLING OF THE LORD JESUS.

Christ dwells in the heart by the Holy Ghost so that there are not two indwellings, but one. And this not figurative or metaphorical, but a literal and glorious reality.

THERE IS THE QUICKENING OF THE MORTAL BODY.

An expression which certainly points to the resurrection, but which may mean some special strength and health imparted to our present mortal bodies, which are the tabernacles and temples of His indwelling.

THERE ARE ALL THE GRACES OF THE SPIRIT.

Which come with linked hands; so that it is impossible to admit one of the golden sisterhood without her introducing all the radiant band. Love brings joy, and joy peace, and peace longsuffering; and similarly through the whole series so that the heart becomes at length tenanted, as was the grave of Christ, with angels.

THERE IS ALSO POWER FOR SERVICE.

No longer timid and frightened, the apostles give their witness with great power. The Gospel comes in power and demonstration through consecrated lips and lives. The very devils are exorcised, and great crowds are bought to the feet of Christ.

This, and much more, is awaiting the moment in life when you shall definitely avail yourself of your privilege and become filled with the Holy Ghost. Then, as time rolls on, you will work great deliverances among people, careless of praise or blame. Perhaps you will know what it is to pass upward to meet Christ in the air. But certainly you will stand beside Him in the regeneration when He shall appear in glory. And then in all the radiant throng there shall be naught to divert your gaze from Jesus, or your thought from the decease (the exodus) which He accomplished at Jerusalem.

And amid the myriads of stars that shall shine forever in the firmament of heaven, not one shall sparkle with more brilliant or more steady glory than Elijah: a man of like passions with ourselves, who through faith subdued kingdoms, wrought righteousness, obtained promises, out of weakness was made strong, waxed valiant in fight, swept to heaven unhurt by death, and stood beside Christ on the transfiguration mount. Prophet of fire, till then, farewell!